INTRODUCTORY NOTICE.

The intemperate course which Mr. O'Connell has chosen to pursue in relation to a large portion of the American People, and his late most unwarrantable attempt to impart the semblance of religious authority, to his incendiary appeals concerning slavery, to his former fellow subjects, now citizens of these United States, have rendered it expedient, in the judgment of many persons, to reprint, together with the recent apostolical letter of the Sovereign Pontiff on the slave trade, the celebrated letters of Bishop England to the Honorable John Forsyth, on domestic slavery, in a form accessible to the great majority of readers.

It is more than probable, that Mr. O'Connell little dreamt of the mischief he was doing, to a still holier cause than that of injured Ireland, when, in the ardour of his vituperation against America, he ventured to misconstrue the Pope's denunciation of the African slave trade (denounced no less by our own and almost every civilized government) into a denial of the compatibility of domestic slavery, as existing in this country, with the practice unto salvation of the Catholic Religion. Still there are many, whom just admiration of his talents and confidence in his many virtues might betray into an inconsiderate adoption of his theological errors; while those unprincipled polemics, who conduct a certain portion of the American press, would eagerly avail themselves of his misstatements, to justify new calumnies against the Church.

To our fellow-citizens of Irish origin, therefore, and the candid and intelligent of every persuasion, these letters on slavery, by the great apostle of this western world, incomplete as they fell from his hurried pen, and sealed by death midway his argument, will yet prove of inestimable value, as exhibiting the true doctrine of Christianity, on the fundamental principle of involuntary servitude, and her ameliorating influences on a state ordained of God, yet liable, like most other social institutions, to manifold and great abuses.

And to *Him* who, forgetful of much that might and ought to have moved him to forbearance, could turn aside unprovoked, from baying the British Lion, to "scatter arrows, firebrands and death" among his most sincere and disinterested well-wishers, this little volume should seem a sad *"memento!"* from the grave of his noblest friend—whose intention it was, as himself assured me (when last my guest in the fall of 1841) that if God permitted him to conclude his essay, it should be

DEDICATED TO DANIEL O'CONNELL!!

WM. GEO. READ.

Baltimore, Dec. 19*th*, 1843.

THE CATHOLIC CHURCH.

DOMESTIC SLAVERY and THE SLAVE TRADE.

THE admirable temper and good sense which characterise the following passages, from the UNITED STATES CATHOLIC MISCELLANY, of December 9th, 1843, fully justify their republication, in connection with the letters which constitute the body of this work.

WE understand that considerable attention has been excited by a document going the rounds of the papers under the title of a "Bull of Pope Gregory XVI, against Slavery," and several inquiries are made as to the meaning of the document and the truth of the charge that the Catholics have concealed or suppressed it in the United States for the last four years.

On recurring to our own files we find that the document itself, not a *Bull*, but an APOSTOLIC LETTER, was published in the *Miscellany* of March 14th, 1840, and that our late lamented bishop, in his two first letters to the Hon. *John Forsyth*, then secretary of state, published likewise in the Miscellany, Oct. 3d and 10th, 1840, fully explained its true meaning. We cannot now say whether it was published in the other Catholic papers of the day, as we have not regular files; but we are under the impression that such was the case. In the acts of the councils of Baltimore, there is a record of its having been formally read and accepted by the prelates in the council of 1840. So much for Catholics concealing or suppressing it. It was likewise given to the public through other channels. It is found, for example, in the Appendix to Mr. Forsyth's address to the people of Georgia on the nomination of General Harrison for the presidency. And yet in just three years it is again trumpeted through the land as something new and hitherto unknown! Truly, we can sometimes be hoaxed.

As to the meaning of the Apostolic Letter, we can see no room for doubt. His Holiness speaks of reducing Indians, Negroes and such others, into slavery; of assisting those who engage in that inhuman traffic, and through desire of gain and to foster their trade, go so far as to excite quarrels and wars among them in their native country. He opposes the continuance of the evil which several of his predecessors, whom he names, endeavored with imperfect success to repress. They speak explicitly of reducing freemen, Indians in South America, and Negroes in Guinea, to slavery. In one word he condemns, what our own laws condemn as felony,—the slave trade. Domestic slavery as it exists in the southern states and in other parts of the Christian world, he does not condemn. This is evident from the tenor of the Apostolic Letter itself, from the declarations made concerning it in Rome, and from the fact that at the fourth provincial council of Baltimore, in which the majority of bishops were from the slaveholding states, it was accepted, without any one's thinking it interfered at all with our domestic polity. We apprehend there is a vast difference between the slave trade and domestic slavery. At least our own laws make the distinction—punishing the one and sanctioning the other. It is absurd then to conclude, that because the Apostólical Letter condemns the piratical slave-trade, it is also aimed against domestic servitude.

There is no danger, no possibility on our own principles, that Catholic theology should ever be tinctured with the fanaticism of abolition. Catholics may and do differ in regard to slavery, and other points of human policy, when considered as ethical or political questions. But our theology is fixed, and is, must be the same now as it was for the first eight or nine centuries of Christianity. During that period, as Bishop England has ably shown in his series of *Letters to the Hon. John Forsyth*, the Church, (Let. xvi,) by the admonitions of her earliest and holiest pastors; by the decrees of her councils made on a variety of occasions; by her synodical condemnation of those who under pretext of religion, would teach the slave to despise his master; by her sanction and support of those laws by which the civil power sought to preserve the rights of the owner; by her own acquiring such property, by deeds of gift or of sale, for the cultivation of her lands, the maintenance of her clergy, the benefit of her monasteries, of her hospitals, of her orphans, and of her other works of charity, repeatedly and evidently testified that she regarded the possession of slave property as fully compatible with the doctrines of the gospel: and this whilst she denounced the pirate who made incursions to reduce into bondage those who were free and unoffending, and regarded with just execration the men who fitted out ships and hired others to engage in the inhuman traffic. In Catholic theology the question is a settled one, and no one would be recognized as a Catholic who would utter the expressions we have heard from the lips of American abolitionists, who called themselves protestants: "If the Bible allows slavery, it should be amended." "The Christianity of the nineteenth century should as far excel the Christianity of the early Church, as that did the old Jewish law," &c.

The line of conduct prescribed especially to the Catholic clergy is laid down by the venerable and learned bishop of Philadelphia in his standard work, *Theologia Moralis*, vol. i, tract. v, cap. vi, and tract. viii, cap. iv. From the first cited chapter we translate the following paragraph.

"37. But what is to be thought of the domestic servitude which exists in most of the southern and western states, where the posterity of those who were brought from Africa, still remain in slavery? It is indeed to be regretted that in the present fullness of liberty in which all glory, there should be so many slaves, and that to guard against their movements, it has been necessary to pass laws prohibiting their education, and in some places greatly restricting their exercise of religion. Nevertheless since such is the state of things, nothing should be attempted against the laws, nor any thing be done or said that would make them bear their yoke unwillingly. But the prudence and the charity of the sacred ministers should appear in their effecting that the slaves, imbued with Christian morals, render service to their masters, venerating God, the supreme Master of all; and that the masters be just and kind, and by their humanity and care for their salvation, endeavour to mitigate the condition of their slaves. The apostles have left us these rules; which if any one should neglect and through a feeling of humanity, endeavor to overturn the entire established order, he would in most cases but aggravate the condition of the slaves. The Pope, in the before mentioned constitution, omitted not to lay this before us. "For the apostles, inspired by the Holy Ghost, taught slaves to obey their temporal masters, as they would Christ himself, and to do the will of God cheerfully : and they also gave a precept to the masters to act kindly towards their slaves, to give them what is just and reasonable, and to refrain from threatening them, knowing that the Lord of both is in heaven, and that with Him there is no acceptation of persons."

How strictly this instruction is complied with, and how beneficial are its effects, is known to every one who has any knowledge of the character of Catholic slaves. They are every where distinguished as a body for orderly habits and fidelity to their masters ; so much so that, in Maryland, where they are numerous, their value is 20 or 25 per cent. above that of others.

We have said this much, not to vindicate the southern clergy of our church from the charge of abolitionism, for we believe it has never been preferred against them, but simply to satisfy the inquiries of some of our fellow citizens, whose attention has been drawn by recent events to this subject.

SANCTISSIMI DOMINI NOSTRI
GREGORII
DIVINA PROVIDENTIA
Papæ XVI.
LITTERÆ APOSTOLICÆ
DE
NIGRITARUM COMMERCIO
NON EXERCENDO.
[*ARMA*.]

ROMÆ: — TYPIS COLLEGII URBANI. — 1840.

GREGORIUS, PP. XVI.
Ad futuram rei memoriam.

In supremo Apostolatus fastigio constituti, et nullis licet suffragantibus meritis gerentes vicem Jesu Christi Dei Filii, qui propter nimiam caritatem suam Homo factus mori etiam pro Mundi redemptione dignatus est, ad Nostram pastoralem sollicitudinem pertinere animadvertimus, ut Fideles ab inhumano Nigritarum seu aliorum quorumcumque hominum mercatu avertere penitus studeamus. Sane cum primum diffundi coepit Evangelii lux, senserunt alleviari plurimum apud Christianos conditionem suam miseri illi, qui tanto tunc numero bellorum praesertim occasione in servitutem durissimam deveniebant. Inspirati enim a divino Spiritu Apostoli servos quidem ipsos docebant obedire dominis carnalibus sicut Christo, et facere voluntatem Dei ex animo; dominis vero praecipiebant ut bene erga servos agerent, et quod justum est et aequum eis praestarent, ac remitterent minas, scientes quia illorum et ipsorum Dominus est in coelis, et personarum acceptio non est apud Eum.* Universim vero cum sincera erga omnes caritas Evangelii Lege summopere commendaretur, et Christus Dominus declarasset habiturum se tamquam factum aut denegatum sibi ipsi quidquid benignitatis et misericordiae minimis et indigentibus praestitum aut negatum fuisset,† facile inde contigit nedum ut Christiani servos suos praesertim Christianos veluti fratrum loco haberent,‡ sed etiam ut proniores essent ad illos qui mererentur libertate donandos; quod quidem occasione imprimis Paschalium Solemnium fieri consuevisse indicat Gregorius Nyssenus.§ Nec defuerunt qui ardentiore caritate excitati se ipsos in vincula conjecerunt, ut alios redimerent; quorum multos se novisse testatur Apostolicus Vir idemque sanctissimae recordationis Praecessor Noster Clemens I.|| Igitur progressu temporis Ethnicarum superstitionum caligine plenius dissipata, et rudiorum quoque populorum moribus Fidei per Caritatem operantis beneficio mitigatis, res eo tandem devenit ut jam a pluribus saeculis nulli apud plurimas Christianorum gentes servi habeantur. Verum, dolentes admodum dicimus, fuerunt subinde ex ipso Fidelium numero qui sordidioris lucri cupidine turpiter obcaecati in dissitis remotisque Terris Indos, Nigritas, miserosve alios in Servitutem redigere, seu instituto ampliatoque commercio eorum, qui captivi facti ab aliis fuerant, indignum horum facinus juvare non dubitarent. Haud sane praetermiserunt plures glor. mem. Romani Pontifices Praecessores Nostri reprehendere graviter pro suo munere illorum rationem, utpote spirituali ipsorum saluti noxiam, et Christiano nomini probrosam; ex qua etiam illud consequi pervidebant, ut infidelium gentes ad veram nostram

* Ad Ephesios VI, 5, seqq., ad Coloss. III, 22. seqq. IV, 1.   † Mathaei XXV, 35, seqq.
‡ Lactantius Divin. Institution. Lib. V, c. 16. Tom. IV, Biblioth. Veterum Patrum Venetiis a Gallandio editae pag. 318.
§ De Resurrect. Domini Orat. III. Tom. III, pag. 420.   Operum edit. Parisiensis Anni 1638.
|| Ad Corinth. Ep. I. cap. 55. Tom. I, Bibl. Galandii p. 35.

Religionem odio habendam magis magisque obfirmarentur. Quo spectant Apostolicae Litterae Pauli III die 29 Maii MDXXXVII, sub Piscatoris Annulo datæ ad Cardinalem Archiepiscopum Toletanum : et aliæ deinceps eisdem ampliores ab Urbano VIII. datæ die 22. Aprilis MDCXXXIX, ad Collectorem Jurium Cameræ Apostolicae in Portugallia ; quibus in Litteris ii nominatim gravissime coercentur, qui Occidentales aut Meridicnales Indos in servitutem redigere, vendere, emere, commutare, vel donare, ab uxoribus et filiis suis separare, rebus et bonis suis spoliare, ad alia loca deducere et transmittere, aut quoquo modo libertate privare, in servitute retinere, nec non praedicta agentibus consilium, auxilium, favorem, et operam quocumque praetextu, et quaesito colore praestare, aut id licitum praedicare, seu docere, ac alias quomodolibet praemissis cooperari auderent seu praesumerent.* Has memoratorum Pontificum Sanctiones confirmavit postmodum et renovavit Benedictus XIV, novis Apostolicis Litteris ad Antistites Brasiliae et aliarum quarumdam Regionum datis die 20. Decembris MDCCXLI., quibus eumdem in finem ipsorum Praesulum sollicitudinem excitavit.† Antea quoque alius his antiquior Praecessor Noster Pius II, quum sua aetate Lusitanorum imperium in Guineam Nigritarum regionem proferretur, Litteras dedit die 7. Octobris MCCCCLXII, ad Episcopum Rubicensem eo profecturum ; in quibus nedum Antistiti ipsi opportunas ad sacrum Ministerium inibi cum majori fructu exercendum facultates impertitus fuit, sed eadem occasione graviter in Christianos illos animadvertit, qui Neophytos in servitutem abstrahebant.‡ Et nostris etiam temporibus Pius VII, eodem, quo sui Decessores, religionis et caritatis spiritu inductus, officia sua apud potentes Viros sedulo interposuit, ut Nigritarum commercium tandem inter Christianos omnino cessaret. Hae quidem Praecessorum Nostrorum Sanctiones et curae profuerunt, Deo bene juvante, non parum Indis aliisque praedictis a crudelitate invadentium, seu a Mercatorum Christianorum cupiditate tutandis ; non ita tamen ut Sancta haec Sedes de pleno suorum in id studiorum exitu laetari posset ; quum immo commercium Nigritarum, etsi nonnulla ex parte imminutum, adhuc tamen a Christianis pluribus exerceatur. Quare nos tantum hojusmodi probrum a cunctis Christianorum finibus avertere cupientes, ac re universa nonnullis etiam Venerabilibus Fratribus Nostris S. R. E. Cardinalibus in consilium adhibitis, mature perpensa, Praedecessorum Nostrorum insistentes vestigiis, Auctoritate Apostolica omnes cujuscumque conditionis Christifideles admonemus et obtestamur in Domino vehementer, ne quis audeat in posterum Indos, Nigritas, seu alios hujusmodi homines injuste vexare, aut spoliare suis bonis, aut in servitutem redigere, vel aliis talia in eos patrantibus auxilium aut favorem praestare ; seu exercere inhumanum illud commercium, quo Nigritae, tamquam si non homines sed pura putaque animantia forent, in servitutem utcumque redacti, sine ullo discrimine, contra justitiae et humanitatis jura, emuntur, venduntur, ac durissimis interdum laboribus exantlandis devoventur, et insuper lucri spe primis Nigritarum occupatoribus per commercium idem proposita, dissidia etiam et perpetua quodammodo in illorum regionibus praelia foventur. Enimvero Nos praedicta omnia, tamquam Christiano nomine prorsus indigna, Auctoritate Apostolica reprobamus ; eademque Auctoritate districte prohibemus atque interdicimus, ne quis Ecclesiasticus aut Laicus ipsum illud Nigritarum commercium veluti licitum sub quovis obtentu aut quaesito colore tueri, aut aliter contra ea, quae nostris hisce Apostolicis Litteris monuimus, praedicare seu quomodolibet publice vel privatim docere praesumat.

Ut autem eaedem hae Nostrae Litterae omnibus facilius innotescant, nec quisquam illarum ignorantiam allegare possit, decernimus et mandamus illas ad valvas Basilicae Principis Apostolorum, et Cancellariae Apostolicae, nec non Curiae Generalis in Monte Citatorio, ac in Acie Campi Florae de Urbe per aliquem ex Cursoribus Nostris, ut moris est, publicari, illarumque exempla ibidem affixa relinqui.

Datum Romae apud S. Mariam Majorem sub Annulo Piscatoris die III. Decembris MDCCCXXXIX. Pontificatus Nostri Anno Nono.

ALOISIUS CARD. LAMBRUSCHINI.

*In Buller. Rom. edit. typis Mainardi Tom VI, part 2; Const. 604, pag. 183.
†In Bullario Benedicti XIV. Tom. I. Const. I. 38.

THE SAME IN ENGLISH.

[N. B.—The translator has aimed at a verbatim rather than graceful translation.]

APOSTOLIC LETTER

OF OUR

MOST HOLY LORD GREGORY XVI,

BY DIVINE PROVIDENCE, POPE:

CONCERNING THE NOT CARRYING ON THE TRADE IN NEGROES.

[*Arms.*]

AT ROME:—BY THE TYPES OF THE URBAN COLLEGE.—1840.

GREGORY XVI, POPE.

For the future memory of the matter.

PLACED at the supreme height of the Apostolate, and although no merits of our own assisting, vicegerents of Jesus Christ, the Son of God, who, by reason of his exceeding great charity, having been made man, hath also vouchsafed to die for the redemption of the world, we consider that it pertaineth to our pastoral solicitude that we should thoroughly endeavor to turn away the faithful from the inhuman traffic in negroes, or any other class of men.

When, indeed, the light of the gospel first began to be diffused, those wretched persons, who, at that time, in such great number went down into the most rigorous slavery, principally by occasion of wars, felt their condition very much alleviated among the Christians. For the apostles, inspired by the divine Spirit, taught, in fact, the slaves themselves to obey their carnal masters as Christ, and to do the will of God from the heart; but they commanded the masters to act well towards their slaves, and to do to them what is just and equal, and to forbear threatenings; knowing that there is a Master both of those and of themselves in the heavens, and that with Him there is no respect of persons.*

Universally, however, since sincere charity to all would most strenuously be recommended by the law of the gospel, and Christ, our Lord, could declare that he would esteem as done or denied to himself whatever of kindness or mercy might be done or denied to the least and to the poor,† it easily ensued therefrom, not only that Christians should regard their slaves, and especially Christians, as brethren,‡ but also that they should be more prone to present with liberty those who might deserve it; which, indeed, Gregory of Nyssa indicates to have been first habitually done on the occasion of the paschal solemnities.§   Nor were wanting

---

* Epist. to Ephes. vi, 5 seqq., Epist. to Colloss. iii, 22 seqq. iv, 1.
† Matth. xxv, 35, seqq.
‡ Lactantius Div. Instit. Lib. v, ch. 16, vol. iv. Collection of the ancient Fathers, edited at Venice, by Gallandius, page 318.
§ 3d Sermon on the Resurrection of the Lord, vol. 3d, page 420, works, Paris edition, 1638.

some who, excited by more ardent charity, cast themselves into chains that they might redeem others,* of whom that apostolic man, our predecessor, Clement I, the same of most holy memory, testifies that he had known many.† Therefore, in the course of time, the darkness of pagan superstitions being more fully dissipated, and the morals also of the ruder nations being softened by means of faith working by charity, the matter progressed so far that now, for many ages, no slaves can be held among many Christian nations. But, grieving much we say it, there were subsequently, from the very number of the faithful, those who, basely blinded by the lust of sordid gain, in remote and distant lands, reduced to slavery Indians, Negroes, or other miserable persons; or, by traffic begun and extended in those who had been made captive by others, did not hesitate to aid the shameful crime of the latter. By no means, indeed, did many Roman Pontiffs of glorious memory, our predecessors, omit severely to rebuke, according to their duty, the conduct of those persons as dangerous to their own spiritual safety, and disgraceful to the Christian name; from which, also, they perceived this to follow, that the nations of infidels would be more and more hardened to hate our true religion. To which refer the apostolic letter of Paul III, of the 29th day of May, 1537, given under the Fisherman's Ring to the cardinal archbishop of Toledo, and another, subsequently, more ample than the former, by Urban VIII, given on the 22d day of April, 1639, to the Collector of the Rights of the Apostolic Chamber in Portugal, in which letter they are by name most severely censured who should dare or presume to reduce to slavery the western or southern Indians, to sell, to buy, to exchange, or give them away, to separate them from their wives and children, or spoil them of their property and goods, to conduct or send them to other places, or in any manner to deprive them of liberty, or retain them in slavery, and also to afford to those who do the aforesaid things, counsel, aid, favor or assistance, upon any pretext or studied excuse, or to preach or teach that it is lawful, or in any other mode to cooperate in the premises.‡ These ordinances of the said pontiffs, Benedict XIV, afterwards confirmed and renewed by a new apostolic letter to the Bishops of Brazil, and of certain other regions, given on the 20th day of December, 1741, by which he excited the solicitude of those prelates to the same end.§ Still earlier, more-

---

* NOTE BY THE TRANSLATOR.—This reference to the Redemptorists has been invidiously *italicised* by a certain profligate transcriber, with the apparent object of insinuating commendation of those abolition agents, or slave stealers, who, (fanatics themselves or hirelings of fanatics,) are engaged in facilitating the escape of runaway slaves from the southern states, and who sometimes, though too seldom, incur the penalties of the violated laws of their country. The candid reader, however, should be informed that there existed, in "the ages of Faith," numerous fraternities of devoted men, who, fortified by previous discipline to encounter the temptations of that state, went into voluntary servitude in exchange for slaves whose freedom they purchased with their own, thus, literally "being made captives by the love of Christ." When abolitionists do this, or any thing like it, we may believe they are led by the "spirit that is first pure, then peaceable," but not till then.

† To Corinth. Epist. 1, chap. 55, vol. 1, Gallandius collection, page 35.
‡ In Bullarium Romanum, printed by Mainard, vol. vi, part 2, const. 604, page 183.
§ In the Bullarium of Benedict xiv, vol. 1, const. 1, 38.

over, another predecessor of ours, more ancient than these, Pius II, when, in his time, the dominion of the Portuguese was extended into Guinea, a region of the negroes, gave a letter on the 7th day of October, 1462, to the bishop of Rubi (?) who was about to proceed thither, in which he not only conferred on that prelate proper faculties for exercising his sacred ministry in that region with greater fruit, but, on the same occasion, animadverted severely against those Christians who dragged the neophytes into slavery.* And, in our times, also, Pius VII, led by the same spirit of religion and charity as his predecessors, sedulously interposed his offices with influential persons, that the traffic in negroes should at length cease entirely among Christians. These ordinances and cares of our predecessors, indeed, by the aid of God, profited not a little in protecting the Indians and other persons aforesaid from the cruelty of invaders or the cupidity of Christian merchants; not so much, however, that this holy see could rejoice in the full success of its efforts in that behalf; since, on the contrary, the traffic in negroes, although in some degree diminished, is yet, hitherto, carried on by many Christians. Wherefore WE, desiring to turn away so great a reproach as this from all the boundaries of Christians, and the whole matter being maturely weighed, certain cardinals of the holy Roman church, our venerable brethren being also called into council, treading in the footsteps of our predecessors, with apostolic authority, do vehemently admonish and adjure in the Lord all believers in Christ, of whatsoever condition, that no one hereafter may dare unjustly to molest Indians, negroes, or other men of this sort; or to spoil them of their goods; or to reduce them to slavery; or to extend help or favor to others who perpetrate such things against them; or to exercise that inhuman trade by which negroes, as if they were not men, but mere animals, howsoever reduced into slavery, are, without any distinction, contrary to the laws of justice and humanity, bought, sold, and doomed sometimes to the most severe and exhausting labors; and, moreover, the hope of gain being by that trade proposed to the first captors of the negroes, dissensions, also, and, as it were, perpetual wars are fomented in their countries. We, indeed, with apostolic authority, do reprobate all the aforesaid actions as utterly unworthy of the Christian name; and, by the same apostolic authority, do strictly prohibit and interdict that any ecclesiastic or lay person shall presume to defend that very trade in negroes as lawful under any pretext or studied excuse, or otherwise to preach, or in any manner, publicly or privately, to teach contrary to those things which WE have charged in this, our Apostolic Letter. But that this, our same letter, may be more easily notorious to all, nor any one may be able to allege ignorance of it, we decree and order it to be published, as is customary, by one of our cursitors, at the doors of the church of the Prince of the Apostles, of the Apostolic Chancery, and of the General Court upon Mount Citorio, and at (the line?) of the Campo di Fiora de urbe, and the copies to be fixed there.

Given at Rome, at St. Mary Major's, under the Fisherman's Ring, on the 3d day of December, 1839, in the ninth year of our pontificate.

ALOISIUS CARDINAL LAMBRUSCHINI.

* Raynald's Ecclesiastical Annals for the year 1462, n. 42.

LETTERS

OF THE LATE

BISHOP ENGLAND TO THE HON. JOHN FORSYTH.

LETTER I.

To the Hon. JOHN FORSYTH, Secretary of State, U. S.

CHARLESTON, *September 29th*, 1840.

SIR,—Your address to the people of Georgia, dated at Fredericksburg, Va., August 29, is now before me. Appended to it is the state of the vote at the Harrisburg convention, by which General Harrison was chosen as the candidate for the presidency, upon whom, the opponents of the present administration had determined to rally. Your object, as you declare in the address, is to show that "he was forced upon the southern portion of [the opposition] by the combination of anti-masonry and *abolitionism.*" The exhibition of the document was intended for this purpose.

In another part of your address you advert to the conduct of Great Britain respecting slaves, and make special reference to two resolutions unanimously adopted by "the World's convention," which met in London in the month of June last, and which you thus describe:—

"Those resolutions denounce the removal of slaves from the old to the new states as an unrighteous traffic, of which 80,000 are annually victims, as exciting detestation. Surprise and abhorrence are acknowledged, that it should be protected and cherished by this government. That it involves hardness of heart in the traders, and cruelty to the negroes, is asserted; and that effectual means should be immediately taken to remove this *stain* from the *character of this nation*. Was there ever such a compound of ignorance, folly and insolence? The brutal O'Connell was quite at home in such a convention; and his insults to the representative of a foreign government near his own, his vituperation of two of our eminent public men, were quite in harmony with the occasion. The transportation of our property from Virginia to Louisiana—the internal slave trade, mark you—is 'unrighteous,' and effectual means ought to be taken in the United States forthwith to remove the *stain* from this nation. What are those means? We can guess. First, prohibition by congress of the transportation of slaves by land or by sea from one state to another; next, a prohibition of the sale of slaves by one man to another in the same state ; and then we shall be ripe for either of the late Mr. Rufus King's or General Harrison's plan of gradual emancipation; the government purchase of the blacks by the proceeds of the public lands, or by the use of the surplus revenue—taxes and duties being properly increased to make that surplus large enough to effectuate the object."

You place the two resolutions in your appendix also. You have in the same address also, the following passage respecting the British government: " The same government has been lately employing itself as the volunteer or selected agent of the Pope in presenting an Apostolic letter on slavery to some of the Spanish American states,—a letter which it is not at all improbable was prepared under influence proceeding from the British isles." And you place this letter upon your appendix. Do I venture a rash opinion, when I say that your object was, to show a union of sentiment, if not a co-operation hostile to southern interests between the abolitionist supporters of General Harrison, the British government, the World's convention, including the brutal O'Connell and his Holiness the Pope ? And that, therefore, all these should be held in fear and detestation by the south?

Though I have had the honor of an interview with you only once, and that several years since at Milledgeville, when you were governor of Georgia, I presume we are sufficiently acquainted, each with the character of the other, to warrant my addressing you not as a stranger. For you personally I have high regard; for your public conduct in many places of trust and honor, I have great respect; the administration in which you hold so prominent a place, has my full confidence : and did I take an active part in politics, it should have my feeble aid.

I have been opposed elsewhere in the performance of the duties of my spiritual office, by the leading abolitionists of the United States, upon the ground of my being a bishop in the southern slave-holding states, and for having reproved Mr. O'Connell's assaults upon our planters, more than eleven years ago : and my judgment and feeling are now what they were then. Yet I do not consider Mr. O'Connell a brute, though I have often told him that his charges were unwarranted and harsh : nor do I think it would be proper to " stop his wind," though I greatly disapprove of his vituperation of our country ; and as regards the anti-slavery folks in Great Britain, you may judge of my attachment to them and my respect for their love of liberty, when I tell you, that for years, whilst I resided in Ireland under the operation of the persecuting code of Britain, I witnessed the yearly display by the anti-slavery society of the preparation and presentation to parliament of two petitions ; one for abolishing the slavery of the negroes in the West Indies, the other for riveting the chains of the white slaves in Ireland, by continuing to enforce the penal laws against the Roman Catholics. Mr. O'Connell at that period, had, as one of his humble associates in the effort to procure the repeal of those laws, the individual who has the honor to address you at present; and frequently has that individual listened with delight to the exciting eloquence in which Mr. O'Connell pourtrayed the sanctimonious hypocrisy of a heartless band, that with words of pity on the lips, with wailing in the tone, with wo upon the visage, and bigotry where the heart should have been, persisted, year succeeding year, in this course, until the Catholic extorted his partial freedom against their will! Mr. O'Connell has not, I hope, more charity than I to forgive those whom God has commanded me to forgive, if I expect pardon for my own sins; but I shall not be found with Mr. O'Connell, banded with men whom I believe to be unchanged in their principles, though not placed in the same circumstances which formerly gave a better opportunity for showing them such as they are.

I have now, sir, reduced our ground of examination to a more narrow space. That space is the letter of the Pope and its circumstances.

I assume you to have insinuated that the letter was written under influences proceeding from the British isles.—Upon what do you build this insinuation? It becomes a man in your position, in such a case to speak out, and to have no reserve. Your position affords ample opportunities of learning the influence at foreign courts. Do you know of any influence which the anti-slavery folks of the British isles had in this case? If you do, you owe it to us of the south in particular to exhibit it, and to let us know its extent, as well as its object.

Now, sir, I am of opinion that British influence has had as little connexion with this letter as Georgian influence had; because, in the first place, this is by no means a novel procedure on the part of the holy see. The Pope tells us, that he did it from a sense of duty. "We deem that it becomes our pastoral solicitude." And though statesmen, in general, pay very little regard to the declaration of motives in state-papers, you will allow me to say that I have had repeated opportunities of satisfying my own mind as to the personal character of the present supreme pontiff, and with me, his declaration of a motive, is conclusive evidence and settles my opinion.

The very tenor of the document shows that he acted not in a novel or unusual course, but in perfect accordance with the principle which influenced the body over which he presides, from its very origin, during successive centuries. Why then seek in British influence a cause for his conduct on the present occasion?

He mentions similar acts of several of his predecessors; Pius II, in 1462, when Edward IV was king of England, and the rival houses of

York and Lancaster gave to the British people other occupation than that of interfering with the Portuguese and the negroes in Africa; Pope Paul III, who wrote in 1537, succeeded Clement VII, in whose pontificate the kingdom of England was separated from the holy see, and it will scarcely be asserted that the Apostolic letter issued by this Pope on the 29th of May of that year, was the result of British influence. You will not say that the British, who in 1639 were regarded as the most virulent opponents of the holy see, had influence, and used it to procure that Pope Urban VIII should issue a similar Apostolic letter on the 22d of April, exactly the day after Charles I, had cast the Lords Brook and Say, into prison, and was so perplexed by the Scotch Covenanters. Nor will you venture to assert that it was British influence procured that a similar Apostolic letter should be issued by Benedict XIV, in 1741, when under George II, the execution of the penal laws against Catholics was in full vigor. And though the anti-slavery societies existed in Great Britian and Ireland during the pontificate of Pius VII, in the first portion of the present century, yet were the penal laws to a considerable extent also in full vigor, and you will scarcely expect us to believe that this society, which presented its annual petition for the persecution of Catholics and the abolition of negro-slavery had great influence with his holiness. Thus, sir, I give you some of the reasons for my opinion that your insinuation against the Pope is wholly without foundation.

I now proceed, sir, to establish another distinction, which I am astonished you could have overlooked. The distinction between the " Slave-Trade," as prohibited by the United States, and the engagement in which would be a high crime, I believe a felony, in any one of their citizens, and the continuance of " domestic slavery" in any of the states by the authority of that state, and with the existence or regulation of which the government of the United States has no concern whatsoever.

The British Anti Slavery Society, Mr. O'Connell and the American abolitionists are equally opposed to both, in all places, and at all times, and they specially wage war upon us at the south for the continuance of this " domestic servitude." The Pope neither mentions nor alludes to this latter in his Apostolic letter which is directed, as were those of his predecessors, solely and exclusively against the former. Yet, sir, you confound his letter with the deeds of the societies, and you use the vague expression, "an Apostolic letter on Slavery," instead of the precise one " against being engaged in the slave trade," which we should expect from so able and experienced a diplomatist, holding for years the high office of secretary of state of these confederated republics.

I should suppose, sir, that to a deeply read and experienced statesman, who has been in Italy, Spain, and I believe other parts of Europe, not merely for idle tour-making, but engaged with courts, on public business, the precise and fixed meaning of the expression "traffic in negroes," would be as familar as " household words," and that Mr. Forsyth would not stand in need of being reminded by me, that in the language of continental Europe, it is precisely and exclusively what the United States knows as criminal trading in slaves: that it is not, at all, applicable to what is known amongst us as " domestic slavery." The Roman Catholic church, which is that of those nations to which I more particularly allude, has always observed this distinction, and it is one as obvious as that which exists between the words " foreign " and " domestic."

The Pope's letter specially describes the traffic, in three places. In one it says, "reduced (in remote lands) Indians, negroes and other unfortunate beings, into slavery." This is the first ingredient in the crime, viz: *reducing those who were free into slavery*, and this in remote lands, which belonged to those so reduced into slavery, and by foreign invaders. The citizens of Georgia have not reduced any such persons into slavery. The letter then designates another class as criminal by becoming accessaries," or the traffic *in those who had been made captive, by others who* did not hesitate to encourage or profit by such unworthy actions ;"—now by the laws of the United States since the year 1808, it would be criminal in one of our citizens to go to Africa and there reduce a negro into slavery, from freedom, or to purchase and ship for a foreign port a negro so enslaved by another, or to introduce him into Georgia or any other place in the United States. This is what is commonly known as the " slave trade " or " traffic in negroes," and this is precisely what these several Popes reprehended and declared to be unlawful.

In the next place it is described by an extract from the letters of Pope Urban VIII, in precisely similar terms, who *reduce into slavery* evidently contemplating persons previously free, and then respecting *the same persons;* that is, those who had been *reduced into* slavery; *buy, sell, exchange,* or *give them away; separate them from their wives and children,* the next expressions could not be, by any effort of ingenuity, used respecting " domestic slaves," such as are in our states, *despoil them of their goods, or possessions,* because in the canon law as well as in the civil law, the *mancipium* or " domestic slave," had no property or possession, except what was permitted to him as a *peculium* or allowance. *Carry or send them to other regions,* which is incompatible with " domestic slavery," but precisely the character of the " slave trade," *or in any manner deprive them of their liberty,* which the domestic slave never had, and of which he could not be deprived; *retain them,* that is, those deprived of their liberty, *in servitude,* &c.

I now proceed to show from the enacting words, if I may use the expression, of the Apostolical letter of his Holiness Pope Gregory XVI, that only the " slave trade " is condemned.

It *admonishes* and *conjures earnestly* in the Lord.—1. Not to molest *unjustly*. 2. Not to despoil of *their goods*. 3. Not to *reduce into slavery*, negroes or any other race of men. 4. Not to render countenance or assistance to those guilty of such practices. 5. Not to be engaged in the sale or purchase, in the inhuman commerce by which negroes are sometimes devoted to intolerable labor. That this commerce is what our laws condemn as the " slave trade," and not that sale and purchase which must frequently occur in domestic slavery, is manifest from the consequence which is described, following as a matter of course from the traffic, "through the love of gain held out to the first possessors of the negroes," that is, the African chieftains ; " dissensions and perpetual wars are fomented throughout the regions which they inhabit,"—and upon all these considerations he prohibits the teaching that " this traffic in negroes," that is, the " slave trade," is lawful.

Thus, sir, it is manifest that you would be equally justified in placing our federal government, under the administration of Mr. Van Buren, and yourself, in company with British and American abolitionists, as you were in placing his holiness Pope Gregory XVI, there. Is it not a little strange, sir, that whilst you exhibit him, and by implication me and my flock, as allied with the abolitionists,—the abolitionists themselves, by a select division to whom it was entrusted in New York, drew up a petition which they forwarded to Hayti for signatures, and which was presented to President Boyer, by the General of Division at Port au Prince, requesting that no communication should be held with me as envoy from this same Pope Gregory XVI, upon the ground that he was not averse to southern slavery, and that I was an enemy to Daniel O'Connell, and an enemy to negroes ? Yes, sir, in a conversation which I held with President Boyer, he acknowledged to me the receipt of the petition, when to spare him the trouble of an examination to discover my sentiments, I informed him that I was aware of the origin and history of the document, and had requested the interview for the purpose of giving him the necessary explanations. He has more common sense than most of the abolitionists, and makes more just allowance for the position of the southern planters than do their fellow-citizens ; and he had the candor and honor to declare that though he must deprecate slavery in every shape, yet from what I told him, he was happy to feel that there were great humanity and very creditable feelings of kindness to their slaves in the great bulk of the southern proprietors, and he added, that he would be devoid of every principle of honor were he to deny the kindness and affection of many of the Spanish proprietors to their slaves in the eastern part of Hayti, previous to the revolution.

This, sir, is the fate of the Catholics of the United States; they are the shuttle cock for the parties of the republics,—threatened by the myrmidons of General Harrison's party to day, and placed in a false position by Mr. Van Buren's secretary of state the next moment. There is, however, sir, one at least of that body who will not submit to the infliction from either one party or the other, from friend or from foe, without endeavoring, however humble his place in the republic, and however powerless his pen, at least to demand more just conduct towards the body to which he has the honor to belong, even though he may not succeed in obtaining what he seeks.

In my next, sir, I shall give additional reasons to show that our holy father, Pope Gregory XVI, is not the associate of the abolitionists, and that the Catholics of the south should not be rendered objects of suspicion to their fellow citizens.

I have the honor to be, sir,

Respectfully,

† JOHN, *Bishop of Charleston.*

LETTER II.

To the Hon. JOHN FORSYTH, Secretary of State, U. S.

Sir—I proceed to give additional reasons to show that the letter of our holy Father, Pope Gregory XVI, regarded only the "slave trade." At the late council in Baltimore, that document was formally read and accepted by the prelates of the United States. Did it contain any thing contrary to their judgment, respecting faith or morals, it would have been their duty to have respectfully sent their statement of such difference to the holy see, together with their reasons for such dissent. Did they believe it contained the correct exposition of Christian morality, and were aware that in the ecclesiastical province of the United States under their charge there existed practices in opposition to that exposition, it would have been their duty to use their best efforts to have such practices discontinued, and to refuse sacraments to those who would persevere in the immoral conduct which it denounced.

Thus, if this document condemned our domestic slavery as an unlawful

and consequently immoral practice, the bishops could not have accepted it
without being bound to refuse the sacraments to all who were slaveholders
unless they manumitted their slaves : yet, if you look to the prelates who
accepted the document, for the acceptation was immediate and unanimous :
you will find, 1st, the Archbishop of Batimore who is also the administrator of Richmond, having charge of the slave-holding territory of the states
of Maryland and Virginia, and the District of Columbia ; 2d, the Bishop of
Bardstown having charge of the slave-holding state of Kentucky ; 3d, the
Bishop of Charleston having charge of the slave-holding states of North Carolina, South Carolina, and Georgia ; 4th, the Bishop of St. Louis having
charge of the slave-holding states of Missouri and Arkansas ; 5th, the
Bishop of Mobile having charge of the slave-holding state of Alabama and
the Territory of Florida ; 6th, the Bishop of New Orleans having charge of
the slave-holding states of Louisiana and Mississippi ; and, 7th, the Bishop
of Nashville having charge of the slave-holding state of Tennessee. They
formed a majority of the council, and were in charge of all the slave-holding portion of the Union. Amongst the most pious and religious of their
flocks, are large slave-holders, who are most exact in performing all their
Christian duties, and who frequently receive the sacraments. The prelates
under whose charge they are, have never, since the day on which they accepted this letter, indicated to them the necessity of, in any manner,
adopting any new rule of conduct respecting their slaves. Nor did the
other six prelates, under whose charge neither slaves nor slave-holders are
found, express to their brethren any new views upon the subject, because
they all regarded the letter as treating of the " slave trade," and not as
touching " domestic slavery."

I believe, sir, we may consider this to be pretty conclusive evidence as
to the light in which that document is viewed by the Roman Catholic
church.

Since the issuing of this document, the holy see has been in treaty with
Portugal, which has, first and last, been most deeply engaged in this cruel
traffic, and I have good reason to believe that one of the stipulations without which the holy see will not conclude the treaty is, that the Portuguese
government will act as ours did upwards of thirty years since, and
prohibit this desolating, criminal, and inhuman system of murder, ruin and
desolation. What southern planter would deliberately sanction a system
of which the following passage of a letter, from a highly creditable person,
is but the description of a trifling appendage ?

" *Sierra Leone, June* 18, 1840.—The slave-trade is by no means extinguished upon this coast; it is, however, more covertly conducted. From
the most accurate sources of information, I can fairly state that not one out

of seven slave-ships is caught by the British cruisers. There is more se-
crecy, but the trade is nearly as frequent as before, but more profitable, and
for that reason more alluring. A few days ago I visited a captured slaver.
In a space which a moderate sized French bedstead would occupy, I have
seen forty-five unhappy wretches packed, without regard to age or constitution, like herrings in a barrel. I saw them fed after they had been captured.
On a shell about the size of a half crown piece, was deposited a pinch of salt,
for which a father and four children contended, each endeavoring to scram-
ble a portion to eat with his rice. I have seen four children packed in a
cask I thought it impossible to contain one."

It is against this desperate traffic, in which Portugal and Spain have had
so enormous a share, that the Pope's letter is directed, and not against domestic slavery, the existence of which he is conscious, but respecting which
he uses no action, and which rests upon a totally different basis, as it is
perfectly unconnected with cruelty such as is above described.

If you will permit myself, sir, to be a witness in this case, I can inform
you, that in different audiences which I had of his Holiness upon the subject of religion in Hayti, I urged, amongst other topics, to induce him to
make a selection of a different person as his envoy, my peculiar position; I
stated that my being a bishop of the diocese within the limits of which was
contained the most numerous negro slave population that is to be found in
any diocess in the world, would render me unacceptable to the Haytian
government, and that being engaged to transact the ecclesiastical organi-
zation of that island would probably render me unacceptable in my own
diocess; his Holiness met me by stating the very distinction to which I
have been drawing your attention. "Though the southern states of your
union have had domestic slavery as an heir-loom, whether they would or
not, they are not engaged in the *Negro traffic*," that is, the "slave trade."

Thus, sir, I trust I have succeeded in showing that this letter of his Holiness which you described to be "an Apostolic letter on Slavery"—does
in fact regard only that "slave trade" which the United States condemn,
and not that domestic slavery which exists in our southern states.

But, sir, I regard this subject as one of great moment at the present time,
and likely to become much more troublesome before many years shall
elapse; I shall therefore enter more deeply upon its elucidation.

Respecting domestic slavery, we distinguish it from the compulsory
slavery of an invaded people in its several degrees. I shall touch upon the
varieties separately. The first is "voluntary;" that which exists amongst
us is not of that description, though I know very many instances where I
have found it to be so; but I regard not the cases of individuals, I look to the
class. In examining the lawfulness of voluntary slavery, we shall test a
principle against which abolitionists contend. They assert generally, that

slavery is contrary to the natural law. The soundness of their position will be tried by enquiring into the lawfulness of holding in slavery a person, who has voluntarily sold himself. Our theological authors lay down a principle, that man in his natural state is master of his own liberty, and may dispose of it as he sees proper; as in the case of a Hebrew, *Exod.* xxi, 5, who preferred remaining with his wife and children as a slave, to going into that freedom to which he had a right; and, as in the case of the Hebrew, *Levit.* xxv, 47, who, by reason of his poverty, would sell himself to a sojourner or to a stranger. Life and its preservation are more valuable than liberty, and hence when Esther addresses Assuerus, vii, 4, she lays down the principle very plainly and naturally. "*For we are sold, I and my people to be destroyed and slain, and to perish. But if we had been sold for bondsmen and bondswomen, I had held my tongue.*" The natural law then does not prohibit a man from bartering his liberty and his services to save his life, to provide for his sustenance, to secure other enjoyments which he prefers to that freedom and to that right to his own labor, which he gives in exchange for life and protection. Nor does the natural law prohibit another man from procuring and bestowing upon him those advantages in return for which he has agreed to bind himself to that other man's service, provided he takes no unjust advantage in the bargain. Thus a state of voluntary slavery is not prohibited by the law of nature; that is, a state in which one man has the dominion over the labor and the ingenuity of another to the end of his life, and consequently in which that labour and ingenuity are the property of him who has the dominion, and are justly applicable to the benefit of the master and not of the slave. All our theologians have from the earliest epoch sustained, that though in a state of pure nature all men are equal, yet the natural law does not prohibit one man from having dominion over the useful action of another as his slave; provided this dominion be obtained by a just title. That one man may voluntarily give this title to another, is plain from the principle exhibited, and from the divine sanction to which I have alluded.

In one point of view, indeed, we may say that the natural law does not establish slavery,—but it does not forbid it, and I doubt how far any of the advocates of abolition would consent to take up for refutation, the following passage of St. Thomas of Aquin,—1, 2, q. 94, a. 5, ad. 2.

" The common possession of all things is said to be of the natural law; because the distinction of possessions and slavery were not introduced by nature, but by the reason of man, for the benefit of human life: and thus the law of nature is not changed by their introduction, but an addition is made thereto."

As well may the wealthy merchant then assert, that it is against the law of nature that one man should possess a larger share of the common fund belonging to the human family for his exclusive benefit, as that it is against the law of nature for one man to be the slave of another. The existence of slavery is considered by our theologians to be as little incompatible with the natural law as is the existence of property. The sole question will be in each case, whether the title on which the dominion is claimed be valid.

I know many slaves who would not accept their freedom; I know some who have refused it; and though our domestic slavery must upon the whole be regarded as involuntary, still the exceptions are not so few as are imagined by strangers.

It may be asked why any one should prefer slavery to freedom. I know many instances where the advantages to the individual are very great; and so, sir, I am confident do you, yet I am not in love with the existence of slavery. I would never aid in establishing it where it did not exist. St. Thomas gives very briefly one of the principles upon which the answer may rest, and Aristotle sustains him (*in* 1 *Polit. c.* 3. *circa fin. T.* 5.) in his view. St. Thomas is proving that the law of nations is distinct from the natural law, and answering an assertion that slavery is of the natural law because some men are naturally fitted for slavery.

" This man is a slave, absolutely speaking, rather a son, not by any natural cause, but by reason of the benefits which are produced, for it is more beneficial to this one to be governed by one who has more wisdom, and to the other to be helped by the labor of the former. Hence the state of slavery belongs principally to the law of nations, and to the natural law only in the second degree, not in the first. 2. 2. q. 57. a. 3. ad. 2.''

The situation of a slave, under a humane master, insures to him, food, raiment and dwelling, together with a variety of little comforts; it relieves him from the apprehensions of neglect in sickness, from all solicitude for the support of his family, and in return, all that is required is fidelity and moderate labor. I do not deny that slavery has its evils, but the above are no despicable benefits. Hence I have known many freedmen who regretted their manumission.

In examining the case of the voluntary slave, sir, we have then discovered some of the grounds upon which Catholic divines, however they may deprecate its existence, teach that slavery is perfectly compatible with the natural law, and that it has been introduced by the law of nations.

It will be useful to draw your attention, sir, to another distinction made by our divines, and which many of our speculative philosophers disregard. The natural state of man in the day of his innocence was very different from that in which he is placed since his fall; and the good gentlemen, in their abstractions, appear to forget the consequences of that original transgression. Death, sickness and a large train of what are now called natural evils, are by Roman Catholics considered to be the consequences of sin. Slavery is an evil and is also a consequence of sin. Thus St. Augustin, bishop of Hippo,

A.D. 425, in his book " Of the city of God," lib. xix, c. 15, informs us that slavery is the consequence of sin. "The condition of slavery is justly regarded as imposed upon the sinner. Hence we never read *slave* in the Scriptures before the just Noe, by this word, punished the sin of his son. Sin, not nature, thus introduced the word."

St. Ambrose, bishop of Milan, A.D. 390, in his book " On Elias and Fasting," c. v. "There would be no slavery to-day, had there not been drunkenness." And St. John Chrysostom, bishop of Constantinople, A.D. 400, Hom. xxix, in Gen. "Behold brethren born of the same mother ; sin makes one of them a servant, and taking away his liberty lays him under subjection." I could multiply quotations, but it is not requisite. Catholic divines are agreed in the principle that the origin of slavery, as of all our infirmities and afflictions, is to be found in sin. Hence it is overlooking one of the essential ingredients in our present condition, for a person who believes in the fall of man, as every Catholic must, to reason upon abstract speculations without taking this important fact into consideration. And besides looking generally at this fact and its results, he should also consider the full force of the sentence, Gen. ix, 25 : " Cursed be Canaan, a servant of servants shall he be unto his brethren." Let him add to this the two succeeding verses, in which Sem and Japeth are promised the service of Canaan. It certainly was not then against the divine law for Sem and Japeth to use the service of Canaan.

Pope Gelasius I, A.D. 491, in his letter to the bishops of the Picene territory, the present march of Ancona, in Italy, writing against the Pelagian heresy, states slavery to have been a consequence of sin, and to have been established by human law. Labbe IV, col. 1176—E. And in the book xix, " On the city of God," chap. 16, St. Augustin argues at length to show that the peace and good order of society, as well as religious duty, demand that the wholesome laws of the state regulating the conduct of slaves, should be conscientiously observed.

Slavery then, sir, is regarded by that church of which the Pope is the presiding officer, not to be incompatible with the natural law, to be the result of sin by Divine dispensation, to have been established by human legislation, and, when the dominion of the slave is justly acquired by the master to be lawful, not only in the sight of the human tribunal, but also in the eye of Heaven : but not so the " slave trade," or the reducing into slavery the African and Indian in the manner that Portugal and Spain sanctioned, which they continue in many instances still to perpetrate, and which the Apostolic letters have justly censured as unlawful.

The distinction will, I trust, be rendered more obvious as I proceed.

I am, sir, respectfully, &c.   † JOHN, *Bishop of Charleston.*
CHARLESTON, S. C., *October 7th,* 1840.

LETTER III.

To the Hon. JOHN FORSYTH, Secretary of State, U. S.

Sir,—I now proceed to examine the titles which divines and canonists have considered to be good and valid for the possession of a slave.

In their definitions and remarks they always restrict that dominion to what is called service of the body, not of the soul, which latter was not held in bondage.

The slave was accountable to God for his morality, and hence the master could not require of him to lay aside the practice of religion or to do an immoral act, but he could command his labor, and was bound to give the necessaries of life.

Bergier very properly remarks—*Dict. Theolog.* Art. *Esclave.* That in the wandering state of early tribes and families where civil society had yet been scarcely, and in only few places, established; a servant could not change his master without expatriation, nor could a master send away his servants without destroying his family, and in this state of things domestic slavery became inevitable. It was, however, he remarks, very greatly mitigated under the patriarchal government, and he instances one great benefit which would accrue, though certainly very seldom to the servant. *Genes.* xv, 2. *And Abram said: Lord God, what wilt thou give me? I shall go without children: and the son of the steward of my house is this Damascus Eliezer.* 3. *And Abram added: but to me thou hast not given seed; and lo my servant born in my house shall be my heir.*

He adds, that civil liberty became a benefit, only after the establishment of civil society, when man had the protection of law, and the multiplied facilities for subsistence: that previous to this absolute freedom would be an injury to a person bereft of flocks, herds, lands, and servants; hence that Abraham and the other patriarchs held great numbers of slaves whom they treated with parental care, and governed by wholesome discipline, and whose services were absolutely the property of their masters.

Job possessed slaves, and he treated them with kindness, xxxi, 13. *If I have despised to abide judgment with my man servant, or my maid servant, when they had controversy against me.* 14. *For what shall I do when God will rise to judge? And when he shall examine what shall I answer him?* 15. *Did not he that made me in the womb, make him also, and did not one and the same form us in the womb?*

How came these patriarchs to have property in those slaves ? Many of them were born in their houses, that is, of their servants, and this was acknowledged to be a good title, not only by the law of nations, but clearly, in the case before us, by the law of God. But how were their parents slaves ? Perhaps originally they voluntarily became so. They might also have been bought from others who had acquired a just dominion by that or by some other good title. I am now only treating of the title which rests on birth, the validity of which the patriarchs thus testified. In *Genesis* xiv, 14, we find Abraham arming three hundred and eighteen of his trained servants born in his house, to accompany him to the rescue of Lot. In ch. xv, we find Eliezer Damascus, his servant born in his house. In ch. xvi, we find Agar the Egyptian a maid or slave of Sarai, whom she introduced as a wife of an inferior rank to Abram. In ch. xxi, we find this bondswoman or slave of Sarai together with her son Ishmael, who was the slave equally as he was the son of Abraham, sent away by the direction of her mistress Sarai, as in chap. xvi, we find that Abraham declared to Sarai, " Behold thy handmaid is in thy own hand, use her as it pleaseth thee." Grotius says that it was a concession of power even to put her to death, and St. John Chrysostom, Hom. 37, describes it as an unlimited power of punishment for petulance and insubordination ; which Calmet in his remarks on this place, says every master had over his slave, and every husband had over the slave of his wife. In ch. xvii, when God is making a covenant with Abraham he recognises the validity of this title to servitude by birth. 12. " He that is born in the house, as well as the bought servant, shall be circumcised." 23. " Then Abraham took Ishmael his son, and all that were born in his house, and all whom he had bought, every male among the men of his house, and he circumcised the flesh of their foreskin forthwith the very same day, as God had commanded him." 27. " And all the men of his house, as well they that were born in his house as the bought servants and strangers, were circumcised with him."

Thus God himself recognised the validity of the title to a slave founded upon purchases as well as upon birth.

The title by donation or gift is equally plain as is that by purchase. *Genes.* xx, 14. " And Abimelech took sheep, and oxen and servants and handmaids, and gave to Abraham." They accompanied their mistress upon marriage. *Gen.* xxiv, 61. We may observe the same in *Gen.* xxx, 43, xxxi, 21.

The titles thus seen are, fair purchase, or gift, and birth.

When Moses led the people from Egypt, the Lord himself gave to him, in the desert, laws not only for morality, but also for the ritual service of religion, and a civil or political code.

I shall dwell very briefly upon this latter:—but I shall previously remark that in the great moral code known as the decalogue, the Almighty recognises the legitimate existence of slavery. *Exod.* xx, 10. " But on the seventh day is the sabbath of the Lord thy God, thou shalt do no work on it, thou nor thy son, nor thy daughter, nor thy *man servant*, nor thy *maid servant*, nor thy beast, nor the stranger that is within thy gates." 17. "Thou shalt not covet thy neighbor's house; neither shalt thou desire his wife, nor his *servant*, nor his *handmaid;* nor his ox, nor his ass, nor any thing that is his."

In the political or civil legislation, of which God himself is the author, we find provision made for.

1. The temporary slavery of a Hebrew. *Ex.* xxi, 2. " If thou buy a Hebrew servant, six years shall he serve thee: and in the seventh he shall go free, for nothing. *Levit.* xxv, 39. If thy brother, constrained by poverty, sell himself to thee, thou shalt not oppress him with the service of bond servants. 40. But he shall be with thee as a hireling and a sojourner: he shall work with thee until the year of the jubilee. 41. And afterwards he shall go out with his children, and shall return to his kindred and the possession of his fathers. 42. For they are my servants, and I brought them out of the land of Egypt: let them not be sold as bondsmen. 43. Afflict him not by might, but fear thy God."

2. Provision was made for his clothing and his family, *Exod.* xxi, 3. " With what raiment he came in, with the like let him go out: if having a wife, his wife shall go out with him." *Lev.* xxv, 41. " He shall go out with his children." Thus the Hebrew could sell only his labor until the year of the jubilee, because God bestowed upon him a special right. 42. His wife and children were free, and Calmet, quoting Selden (li. 6, c. I, de jure nat. et gent.) states that the master was obliged to support the family.

3. Provision was made for his relief at the time of completing his servitude. *Deut.* xv, 1. " In the seventh year thou shalt make a remission." 12. "When thy brother, a Hebrew man, or a Hebrew woman is sold to thee, and hath served thee six years, in the seventh thou shalt let him go free." 13. " And when thou sendest him out free, thou shalt not let him go away empty." 14. "But shalt give him for his way, out of thy flock, and out of thy barn floor, and thy wine press wherewith the Lord thy God shall bless thee." 15. " Remember that thou also wast a bond servant in the land of Egypt, and the Lord thy God made thee free; and therefore I now command thee this." 18. " Turn not away thy eyes from them when thou makest them free: because he hath served thee six years according to the wages of a hireling: that the Lord thy God may bless thee in all the works thou dost."

4. Provision was made for the case of his marrying a slave. *Exod.* xxi, 4.

"But if his master give him a wife, and she hath borne him sons and daughters, the woman and her children shall be her master's ; but he himself shall go out with his raiment."

5. Provision was made for the man's continuance in servitude, should he prefer it to his liberty, in order to remain with his enslaved wife and children.—*Exod.* xxi, 5. "And if the servant shall say : I love my master : and my wife and children. I will not go out free." 6. "His master shall bring him to the gods (judges), and he shall be set to the door and the posts, and he shall bore his ear through with an awl : and he shall be his servant for ever."—*Deut.* xv, 19. "But if he say : I will not depart : because he loveth thee and thy house, and findeth that he is well with thee : 17. Thou shalt take an awl and bore through his ear in the door of thy house ; and he shall serve thee for ever : thou shalt do in like manner to thy woman servant also."

6. Provision was made for the case of a Hebrew who sold himself in servitude to a stranger. The desire of the great legislator of this people was, to keep them separate from the other nations, and especially to preserve the integrity of their religion, by preventing their falling under the dominion of the idolatrous people by whom they were surrounded. Hence the greatest care was taken to prevent servitude to strangers, and to facilitate, without injustice, the redemption of those who became its subjects. Thus it was regulated. *Lev.* xxv, 47. "If the hand of a stranger or a sojourner grow strong among you, and thy brother being impoverished sell himself to him or to any of his race." 48. "After the sale, he may be redeemed. He that will of his brethren may redeem him." The following verses show the power the servant had of redeeming himself, by paying at the rate of the hire of a servant, in the ratio of the time to the jubilee. And an injunction was given not to permit the stranger to treat him with cruelty ; at all events he was to be free in the year of the jubilee.

7. Provision was made for fugitive slaves under peculiar circumstances. *Deut.* xxiii, 15, 16.

8. Hebrew parents were permitted under certain circumstances to sell their children to their own brethren. Special provisions are made for the treatment of young females thus sold. *Exod.* xxi, 7. She was to be treated differently from a bondwoman. 8. The buyer could sell her, but not to a oreigner. 9. If his son marries her, she shall be treated as his daughter. 10. If she be set aside for another wife, she must be fully provided for. 11. Should there be a neglect of any of these conditions, she became free.

9. The Hebrews were allowed to have foreigners and their descendants in perpetual slavery. *Levit.* xxv, 44. "Let your bondmen and bondwomen be of the nations that are round about you." 45. "And of the strangers that

sojourn among you, or those that were born of them in your land, these you shall have for servants." 49. "And by right of inheritance, shall leave them to your posterity, and shall possess them for ever."

10. Where slavery did not exist, there could not be the crime which is made capital in *Exodus* xxi, 16. " He that shall steal a man and sell him, being convicted of the guilt, shall be put to death," and in *Deut.* xiv, 7, " If any man be found soliciting his brother of the children of Israel, and selling him, shall take a price, he shall be put to death, and thou shalt take away the evil from the midst of thee."

11. The excesses of masters in the punishment of slaves were provided against by the law in *Exod.* xxi, v. 20 and 21. " He that striketh his bondman or bondwoman with a rod, and they die under his hands, shall be guilty of the crime. But if the party remain alive a day or two, he shall not be subject to the punishment, because it is his money." * And again in v. 26 and 27. " If any man strike the eye of his man servant or maid servant and leave them but one eye, he shall let them go free for the eye which he put out. Also if he strike a tooth out of his man servant or his maid servant, he shall in like manner make them free."

12. Compensation was provided for the masters whose slaves had been injured. *Exod.* xxi. Of a wicked ox that was known to be dangerous, 52. " If he assault a bondsman or bondswoman, *the owner of the ox*, shall give thirty sicles of silver (the usual price of an ordinary slave) to their master, and the ox shall be stoned."

13. In the precepts relating to the observance of religious ceremonies as well as respecting the sabbath, the eternal Lawgiver draws the distinction between the free and the slave.—*Deut.* xii, 11. " In the place which the Lord your God shall choose, that his name may be therein. Thither shall you bring all the things that I command you, holocausts and victims and tithes and the first fruits of your hands, and whatsoever is the choicest in the gifts which you shall vow to the Lord." 12. " There shall you feast before the Lord your God, you, and your sons and your daughters, your men servants and your maid servants, and the Levite that dwelleth in your cities." The same distinction is repeated in v. 18, and in *Deut.* xxi, 11, 14.

I may now enumerate several titles of dominion plainly expressed, or manifestly adverted to in this code emanating from God himself.

1. A man disposes of his own liberty.—*Exod.* xxi, 5. *Levit.* xxv, 39. *Deut.* xv, 15.—I am aware that Judge Blackstone and Montesquieu appear to contend against the right of any man to sacrifice his liberty. It is by assuming the existence of a parallelism which does not exist, viz : that liberty is an equal good with life, and because man has not the power of disposing of the latter, he has therefore no power to dispose of the former.

The divine legislation of the Hebrews is, however, quite decisive.

2. A person is born in servitude.—*Exod.* xxi, 4.—*Levit.* xxv, 45, 46.

3. Children sold by their parents.—*Exod.* xvi, 7.—*Isa.* l, 1.

4. Thieves unable to make restitution and pay the penalty legally in- flicted. *Exod.* xxii, S.

5. We find that a creditor could also take his debtor or his children to serve for the redemption of the debt. IV, or II *Kings*, chap. iv.

6. Purchase is recognised throughout as a good title to the services of one already enslaved.

7. Slaves were made in war.—*Deut.* xx, v. 14.

Thus, sir, all the divines of the Roman Catholic church acknowledge that they find in the divine legislation for the Hebrew people the recogni- tion of slavery and the enactment of provisions for its regulation.

It was not contrary to the law of nature or else the God of nature could not have permitted its sanction in that code which he gave to his chosen people. It was not incompatible with the practice of pure and undefiled religion, because it was, at least, permitted by him who is the great and sole object of the highest religious homage. It was in many cases rather a source of protection than of evil to its unfortunate subjects.

St. Augustin, as I before remarked, in my last, stated that slavery was a consequence of sin. (lib. xix, De civitate Dei. cap. 15.) Not that the sinful individual is always the slave, but that this evil was inflicted upon a sinful world, as were sickness, war, famine, &c. whereby it often happens that the less sinful are afflicted, that they may by such chastisement be turned more to the service of God and brought to his enjoyment. He re- fers to the example of Daniel and his companions in the Babylonian capti- vity, whereby Israel was brought to repentance. And he shows from the etymology of the name *Servus*, that according to the law of nations at the time, the conqueror had at his disposal the lives of his captives, some of whom were *servati* or *servi*, that is, kept from destruction, and their lives spared upon the condition of doing works of laborious drudgery for their masters.

In his chap. 16, he shows the distinction in bodily employment and labor between the son and the servant : but as regards the soul, each was equally under the master's care and deserved a like protection. Hence the masters were called *Patres Familias* or " Fathers of the Household," to show that they should consult for the eternal welfare of their slaves as a father for that of his children. And he insists upon the right and obligation of the master to restrain his slaves from vice, to preserve due discipline, to govern with firmness and yet with affection. And not only by verbal correction, but if unfortunately it should be requisite with moderate, corporal chastisement, not merely for the punishment of delinquency, but also for a salutary monition to others. He proceeds still farther to show that it is a public duty, because the peace of a vicinage depends upon the good order of its families, and the safety of a state depends upon peace and discipline of all the vicinages within its precincts.

Thus he exhibits the principles that pervaded the code given by God himself to the Hebrew people.

I shall continue, sir, to treat the progress of legitimate slavery in its subsequent history.

I have the honor to be, sir,

Respectfully, &c.

† JOHN, *Bishop of Charleston.*

CHARLESTON, S. C., *October 13th,* 1840.

LETTER IV.

To THE HON. JOHN FORSYTH, SECRETARY OF STATE, U. S.

SIR—The divine sanction for the existence of slavery and for the various titles by which property in slaves may be acquired, being shown, it would rest upon those who deny its religious legality to-day, to prove distinctly that this sanction had been withdrawn. Nor would it answer their purpose to plead that the political and civil code of Judea was not to be obligatory upon Christians; because we do not assert their obligation upon us; but we declare that they contained no sanction incompatible with the natural law or the principles of sound morality; and they did contain the sanction of slavery and of the titles of acquisition, which we say, cannot therefore be immoral, unless they be incompatible with laws subsequently enacted. This enactment is to be proved by those who oppose us, and must be at least as plain as what we have exhibited.

The view which I have taken was confined to Judea, because it was only there I could procure distinct and direct evidence of the divine sanction. Nor was this a privilege of that people, because we find it in existence previous to the formation of the Hebrew nation. Abimelec, the cotemporary of their great progenitor, gave slaves to Abraham; and as he could not convey a better title than existed in himself, if he did not lawfully own the slaves, Abraham could not lawfully accept them. Bathuel was not a Hebrew, and he had slaves, some of whom accompanied his daughter Rebecca. Laban was not a Hebrew, nor was Job. It was not then a privilege granted to the Hebrew people, nor to Abraham and his progeny, but it was a common right, and subject to the legislative regulation of nations.

Its existence was very extensive, if not universal, and the regulations concerning it varied in the several states and nations. The exhibition of their difference would be an idle and useless display of references to the various codes and customs of the Gentile world. The number of slaves was very great. In Attica at one period when the citizens did not amount to thirty thousand, the slaves were four hundred thousand : this disparity in numbers was not, however, a fair representation of the world, nor even of Greece itself. The generally acknowledged titles, by the law of nations, were purchase, birth, legal conviction, or capture in just war.

It will be well to observe in this place, and the principle will be of essential importance in examining the Apostolical letters of the holy see, that war waged for that mere pretext of making slaves ; or under other pretexts, but for that purpose, was always considered to be as notoriously piratical as would be incursions made for the purpose of obtaining any other booty ; nay, in this case it was worse than any other kind of robbery. The stealing of freemen and selling them into slavery or invading a people for the purpose of reducing them to slavery, were considered great crimes ; the individuals who were thus guilty were in almost every place liable to capital punishment ; and if a nation committed the crime, it was considered to have lost its rank of civilization. The capture should have been made in war properly waged, and carried on according to the usage of civilized nations : and in most cases the captive could, if he had property, redeem himself or be ransomed by his friends, and thus saved from slavery.

Any person conversant with the history of the Gentile nations, previous to the Christian epoch, will immediately perceive the striking contrast between the comparatively happy situation of the slaves of the Hebrews, and the oppression under which those of the most polished amongst the other nations labored. Yet the writings of some of these latter servants form no inconsiderable share of our classical collections.

I shall then pass over any view of the slave system of the Gentiles farther than to remark, that at the period when the Saviour came it was exceedingly oppressive, and that in many instances the master could put his slave to death without the interference of any legal tribunal, and that the instances of its infliction were by no means rare. I shall not stop to inquire into the validity of the claim to the exercise of this power, nor into the moral criminality of those who use it.

I proceed to examine what the divine legislator of Christianity has done upon this subject.

He made no special law either to repeal or to modify the former and still subsisting right; but he enforced principles, that by their necessary operation and gradual influence, produced an extensive amelioration. In the words of the Apostolic letter of Pope Gregory XVI.—"Verily, when the light of the Gospel first began to diffuse itself, those unfortunate men, who, by occasion of so many wars, had fallen into cruel servitude, felt their condition among Christians very much alleviated. Inspired, indeed, by the Divine Spirit, the apostles taught servants to render obedience to their masters in the flesh, as unto Christ, and to do the will of God with a cheerful mind; yet they commanded also unto masters that they should use their servants kindly, that they should render unto them what is just and right, and that they should not employ threats, remembering that the God of both is in heaven, and that with Him there is no respect of persons."

Bergier says, *Dict. Theol. Art. Esclavage III.* "When our Lord Jesus Christ appeared upon earth, the rights of humanity were not better known than they were in the time of Moses. The philosophers, in place of rendering them more clear had made them more obscure. The Greeks had decided that amongst men, some nations were born for liberty, and others for slavery. That every thing was lawful against Barbarians, that is, against every one that was not a Greek. In the state of Athens alone, there were four hundred thousand *slaves* for twenty thousand citizens. In Rome the condition of slaves was not better than that of beasts of burthen. One shudders at reading the treatment of those unfortunates. (See *Memoirs of the Academy of Inscriptions*, tom. 63, in 12mo. p. 102). Such was the common law of all nations in the ages of philosophy. If Jesus Christ had by his laws attacked, face to face, this assumed right, he would have given weight to the opposition of the emperors and other sovereigns to the promulgation of the gospel: and our philosophers of the present day would have accused him for having assailed the public law of all nations."

"The divine legislator did better, he disposed the minds of people, by his maxims of charity, of meekness, of fraternal love between men, to perceive that slavery in its then character was getting into opposition to the natural law. It may be perceived by the letter of St. Paul to Philemon, what was the teaching of the gospel morality on this essential point, and how eloquent was the language of humanity proceeding from the lips of Christian charity. The baptized slave became of right the brother of his master."

The right which Bergier in this place alludes to, as his entire article shows, was not a civil but a religious right, the right of brotherhood in

Christ Jesus, as redeemed by him and an heir to the same glorious inheritance, as the Apostle St. Paul describes it in his epistle to the Galatians, chap. vii, 26. "For you are all children of God, by faith in Christ Jesus." 27. "For as many of you as have been baptized in Christ, have put on Christ." 28. "There is neither Jew nor Greek: there is neither bond nor free; there is neither male nor female. For you are all one in Christ Jesus." 29. "And if you be Christ's, then you are the seed of Abraham; heirs according to the promise."

In the New Testament we find instances of pious and good men having slaves, and in no case do we find the Saviour imputing it to them as a crime, or requiring their servants' emancipation.—In chap. viii, of St. Matthew, we read of a centurion, who addressing the Lord Jesus, said, v. 9, "For I also am a man under authority, having soldiers under me, and I say to this man, go, and he goeth: and to another, come, and he cometh: and to my servant, do this and he doth it." v. 10. "And Jesus hearing this wondered, and said to those that followed him : Amen, I say to you, I have not found so great faith in Israel." * * v. 13. And Jesus said to the centurion, go, and as thou hast believed, so be it done to thee. And the servant was healed at the same hour." St. Luke, in ch. vii, relates also the testimony which the ancients of Israel gave of this stranger's virtue, and how he loved their nation, and built a synagogue for them.

In many of his parables, the Saviour describes the master and his servants in a variety of ways, without any condemnation or censure of slavery. In Luke xvii, he describes the usual mode of acting towards slaves as the very basis upon which he teaches one of the most useful lessons of Christian virtue, v. 7. "But which of you having a servant ploughing or feeding cattle, will say to him, when he is come from the field, immediately, go sit down." 8. "And will not rather say to him, make ready my supper, and gird thyself, and serve me while I eat and drink, and afterwards, thou shalt eat and drink ?" 9. "Doth he thank that servant because he did the things that were commanded him ?" 10. " I think not. So you also, when you shall have done all the things that are commanded you, say : we are unprofitable servants, we have done that which we ought to do."

After the promulgation of the Christian religion by the apostles, the slave was not told by them that he was in a state of unchristian durance. 1. Cor. vii, 20. "Let every man abide in the same calling in which he was called." 21. "Art thou called being a bond-man ? Care not for it ; but if thou mayest be made free, use it rather." 22. "For he that is called in the Lord, being a bond-man, is the free-man of the Lord. Likewise he that is called being free, is the bond-man of Christ." 23. "You are

bought with a price, be not made the bond-slaves of men." 24. "Brethren, let every man, wherein he was called, therein abide with God." Thus
a man by becoming a Christian was not either made free nor told that he
was free, but he was advised, if he could lawfully procure his freedom, to
prefer it to slavery. The 23d verse has exactly that meaning which we
find expressed also in chap. vi, v. 20. "For you are bought with a great
price, glorify and bear God in your body, which is addressed to the free
as well as to the slave: all are the servants of God, and should not be
drawn from his service by the devices of men, but should "walk worthy of
the vocation in which they are called." Eph. iv, i. and the price by which
their souls, (not their bodies) were redeemed, is also described by St. Peter I, c. i, 10. "Knowing that you were not redeemed with corruptible
gold or silver from your vain conversation of the tradition of your fathers."
19. "But with the precious blood of Christ, as of a lamb unspotted and
undefiled."—That it was a spiritual redemption and a spiritual service, St.
Paul again shows, Heb. ix, 14. "How much more shall the blood of Christ,
who through the Holy Ghost, offered himself without spot to God, cleanse
our conscience from dead works to serve the living God?" It is then a
spiritual equality as was before remarked, in the words of St. Paul, 1 Cor.
xii, 13. "For in one spirit we are baptized into one body, whether Jews or
Gentiles, whether bond or free." And in the same chapter he expatiates
to show that though all members of the one mystical body, their places,
their duties, their gifts are various and different. And in his epistle to the
Galatians, chap. iv. he exhibits the great truth which he desires to inculcate by an illustration taken from the institutions of slavery, and without
a single expression of their censure.

Nor did the apostles consider the Christian master obliged to liberate
his Christian servant. St. Paul in his epistle to Philemon acknowledges
the right of the master to the services of his slave for whom however he
asks, as a special favor, pardon for having deserted his owner. 10. "I
beseech thee for my son Onesimus whom I have begotten in my chains."
11. "Who was heretofore unprofitable to thee, but now profitable both to
thee and to thee." 12. "Whom I have sent back to thee. And do thou
receive him as my own bowels." Thus a runaway slave still belonged to
his master, and though having become a Christian, so far from being thereby liberated from service, he was bound to return thereto and submit himself to his owner. In the same manner that St. Paul sent Onesimus did
the angel send Agar. Gen. xvi, 6. "And when Sarai afflicted her she ran
away." 7. "And the angel of the Lord having found her by a fountain
of water in the wilderness, which is in the way to Hur in the desert." 8.
He said to her: Agar, hand-maid of Sarai, whence comest thou? and

whither goest thou ? And she answered : I flee from the face of Sarai, my mistress." 9. "And the Angel of the Lord said to her : return to thy mistress, and humble thyself under her hand."

St. Paul, indeed, in v. 8 says, "though I might have much confidence in, Christ Jesus to command thee that which is to the purpose." It was the command of friendship and upon the plea of gratitude as he exhibits in v. 19. "Not to say to thee that thou owest me thy own self also;" because of the conversion and instruction of Philemon by the apostle,—and the friendship is exhibited in v. 22. "But withal prepare me also a lodging : for I hope through your prayers I shall be given unto you," still the apostle felt that even notwithstanding all those grounds the right of Philemon subsisted unimpaired. 13. "Whom I would have detained with me, that he might have ministered to me in the bonds of the Gospel." 14. "But without thy counsel I would do nothing, that thy good deed might not be as it were of necessity but voluntary."—It is true that in v. 16, the apostle requests his manumission, but in v. 18 he exhibits his readiness to pay his ransom if required. "And if he hath wronged thee in any thing or is in thy debt, put it to my account." And he makes himself legally responsible. 19. "I Paul have written with my own hand, I will repay it." Philemon acceded to the request of St. Paul, forgave Onesimus and sent him to Rome to serve the apostle, from whom he received his freedom, and was one of the bearers of the letter to the Colossians. Col. iv, 9,

Again it is manifest from the Epistle of St. Paul to Timothy that the title of the master continued good to his slave though both should be Christians, c. vii. "Whosoever are servants under the yoke, let them count their masters worthy of all honor, lest the name and doctrine of the Lord be blasphemed." 2. "But they who have believing masters, let them not despise them because they are brethren, but serve them the rather, because they are faithful and beloved, who are partakers of the benefit. These things exhort and teach." And in the subsequent part he declares the contrary teaching to be against the sound words of Jesus Christ, and to spring from ignorant pride.

Slaves are still farther urged by the apostle to due obedience, in his epistle to the Ephesians, c. vi, 5. "Servants obey your carnal masters with fear and trembling, in the simplicity of your heart, as Christ. 6. "Not serving to the eye, as it were pleasing men, but as the servants of Christ doing the will of God from the heart." 7. "With a good will doing service to the Lord, and not to men." 8. "Knowing that whatsoever good every one shall do, the same shall he receive from the Lord, whether he be bond or free." And again in his epistle to the Colossians, ch. iii, 22. "Servants, obey in all things your masters according to the flesh, not serv-

ing with the eye, as pleasing men, but in simplicity of heart, fearing God."
22. "Whatever you do, do it from the heart, as to the Lord, and not to
men." 24. "Knowing that you shall receive of the Lord the reward of
inheritance. Serve ye the Lord Jesus Christ." 25. "For he that doth
an injury, shall receive for that which he hath done unjustly, and there is
no respect of persons with God."

The apostle St. Peter, quite aware of the great temptation to impatience
and obstinacy which the misconduct of the master, not seldom, threw in
the way of the servant, enters at considerable length and urges the most
powerful motives to the Christian slave to induce him by the example and
grace of the Saviour, to be patient.—I Peter ii, 18. " Servants be subject to your masters with all fear, not only to the good and gentle, but also to the froward." 19. "For this is thankworthy, if for conscience towards God, a man endure sorrows, suffering wrongfully." 20. "For what
glory is it, if sinning and being buffetted you suffer it? But if doing well
you suffer patiently, this is thankworthy before God." 21. "For unto
this you have been called; because Christ also suffered for us, leaving you
an example that you should follow his steps." 22. "Who did no sin,
neither was guile found in his mouth." 23. "Who when he was reviled
did not revile: when he suffered, he threatened not: but delivered himself
to him that judged him unjustly." 24. " Who himself bore our sins in his
own body upon the tree: that we being dead to sins, should live to justice;
by whose stripes you were healed." 25. " For you were as sheep going
astray: but you are now converted to the pastor and bishop of your souls."

Erasmus says that Cicero never wrote with greater eloquence than did
St. Paul in the epistle to Philemon :—And we may both add, that never
was there a more touching appeal to worried servants than this address of
the prince of the apostles. Thus each apostle besought one class, recom-
mending mercy and kindness to the master; obedience, fidelity and affection to the slave.

It will now fully establish what will be necessary to perfect the view
which I desire to give, if I can show that masters who were Christians were
not required to emancipate their slaves, but had pointed out the duties which
they were bound as masters to perform, because this will show under the
Christian dispensation the legal, moral and religious existence of slave and
master.

The apostle, as we have previously seen, 1 *Tim.* vi, 2, wrote of slaves
who had believing or Christian masters. The inspired penman did not
address his instructions and exhortations to masters who were not of the
household of the Faith. 1 *Cor.* v, 12. " For what have I to do, to judge
them that are without?" 13. " For them that are without, God will judge;

take away the evil one from amongst yourselves." Thus when he addresses masters ; they are Christian masters. Ephes. vi, 9. "And you, masters, do the same things to them (servants) forbearing threatenings, knowing that the Lord both of them and you is in heaven : and there is no respect of persons with him,"—and again, Colos. iv, i, "Masters do to your servants that which is just and equal : knowing that you also have a master in heaven."

We have then in the teaching of the apostles nothing which contradicts the law of Moses, but we have much which corrects the cruelty of the Pagan practice. The exhibition which is presented to us is one of a cheering and of an elevated character. It is true that the state of slavery is continued under the legal sanction, but the slave is taught from the most powerful motives to be faithful, patient, obedient and contented, and the master is taught that though despotism may pass unpunished on earth it will be examined into at the bar of heaven : and though the slave owes him bodily service, yet that the soul of this drudge, having been purchased at the same price as his own, and sanctified by the same law of regeneration, he who is his slave according to the flesh, is his brother according to the spirit.—His humanity, his charity, his affection are enlisted and interested, and he feels that his own father is also, the father of his slave, hence though the servant must readily and cheerfully pay him homage and perform his behests on earth, yet, they may be on an equality in heaven.

How striking, sir, is the contrast between the slave under paganism and the slave under Christianity ? The one dreads only him who can kill the body and then has no more power ; the other fears him who having slain the body, can cast both body and soul into hell fire.

The fear of the Lord becomes the safeguard of society, the shield of the owner, and the support of the owned. The example of the Saviour is the best monition to him who governs to do so with tenderness, affection and charity, blended with wholesome discipline and necessary restraint ; whilst to the governed it is the most impressive lesson of resignation to the divine will, the most effectual exhortation to patient obedience, and the best direction to the attainment of lasting peace and high happiness.

The unfortunate Pagan saw no prospect beyond the grave of a recompense for humility, for submission and for obedience. Nor did his master understand the value of a soul, the nature of beatitude, or the merit of mercy : he saw stern despotism, reckless ambition and proud and unfeeling oppression deified, and in the treatment of his slaves he emulated his gods ; whilst his unfortunate servant crouched before a tyrant whom he hated, and desired the ruin of one from whom he received little kindness.

To the Christian slave was exhibited the humiliation of an incarnate

God, the suffering of an unoffending victim, the invitation of this model of perfection to that meekness, that humility, that peaceful spirit, that charity and forgiveness of injuries which constitute the glorious beatitudes. He was shown the advantage of suffering, the reward of patience, and the narrow road along whose rugged ascents he was to bear the cross, walking in the footsteps of his Saviour. The curtains which divide both worlds were raised as he advanced, and he beheld Lazarus in the bosom of Abraham, whilst the rich man vainly cried to have this once miserable beggar allowed to dip the tip of his finger in water and touch it to his tongue, for he was tormented in that flame.

Thus, sir, did the legislator of Christianity, whilst he admitted the legality of slavery, render the master merciful, and the slave faithful, obedient and religious, looking for his freedom in that region, where alone true and lasting enjoyment can be found.

I shall proceed, sir, to select a few of the many evidences which the intermediate ages furnish, to show the continued legality of domestic slavery, and to exhibit its perfect compatibility with the sound principles of the Christian moral code,—adducing the evidence from the records of that church over which Pope Gregory XVI, so happily presides, and thus conclusively showing that in his Apostolic letter he does not condemn it as immoral or illegal; because the Pope is the divinely constituted and authorized witness of the doctrine and morality of the unchanging church, and not a despot who can alter that teaching at his mere will; whilst the church herself claims no power either to add to the deposit of faith, or to change the principles of that morality for whose promulgation she is divinely commissioned.

I have the honor to be, sir,

Respectfully, &c.

† JOHN, *Bishop of Charleston.*

CHARLESTON, S. C., *October 21, 1840.*

LETTER V

To THE HON JOHN FORSYTH, SECRETARY OF STATE, U. S.

SIR—I have shown that the Saviour did not repeal the permission to hold slaves; but that he promulgated principles calculated to improve their condition, and perhaps, in the process of time, to extinguish slavery. I now proceed to show, from a variety of ecclesiastical documents, that the church which he commissioned to teach all nations, all days to the end of the world, has at all times considered the existence of slaves as compatible with religious profession and practice. Indeed, I might at once conclude, by the general exhibition of the existence of slavery in the midst of Christianity, and the recognition of the right of the Christian master to hold this species of property; but, sir, this is a topic of so much growing importance, that I prefer entering into some detail to establish the evidence more perfectly by such an exhibition as will remove the last shades of doubt.

I am more perplexed at the difficulty of selecting from the mass that lies before me, than I should be in transcribing at length the immense accumulation itself. I shall then show the canonical legislation of that church during a series of ages, in every region, predicated upon the legal and correctly moral existence of the relation of master and slave.

We have seen already in my fourth letter, that in the canonical epistles of St. Peter and of St. Paul, this relation was recognized and regulated by religious provisions.

The apostles held several councils, whose acts are not fully recorded in the relation made by St. Luke, generally known as " Acts of the Apostles." And a very ancient compilation under the title of " Canons of the Apostles," has been known in the church, and if not the authentic record of their enactments, is admitted to be in conformity with the earliest Christian practice. Amongst these the Canon lxxxi, is the following :

Servos in clerum provehi sine voluntate dominorum, non permittimus, ad eorum qui possident molestiam, domorum enim eversionem talia efficiunt. Siquando autem, etiam dignus servus visus sit, qui ad gradum eligatur, qualis noster quoque Onesimus visus est, et domini concesserint ac liberaverint, et œdibus emiserint, fiat.

We do not permit slaves to be raised to clerical rank without the will of their masters, to the injury of their owners. For such conduct produces the upturning of houses. But if, at any time, even a slave may be seen worthy to be raised to that degree as even our Onesimus was, and the masters shall have granted and given freedom, and have sent them forth from their houses, let it be done.

This is the first of a series of similar enactments, and it should be observed that it recognises the principle of the perfect dominion of the master, the injury to his property, and requires the very legal formality by which the slave was liberated and fully emancipated (sending him forth from the house) should be observed.

The slave had the title, without his owner's consent, to the common rights of religion and the necessary sacraments. In using these no injury was done to the property of his owner; but he had no claim to those privileges of religion by acquiring which a certain rank would be obtained, which would diminish his value to the owner, or would degrade the dignity conferred, and which would impose duties that could not be performed without occupying that time upon which his owner had a claim.

There are eight other books of a remote antiquity known as "The Constitutions ascribed to the Apostles," said to be compiled by Pope Clement I, who was a companion of the apostles. It is, however, generally believed that, though Pope Clement might have commenced such a compilation; he did not leave it in the form which it holds to-day, but, like the Canons of the Apostles, the exhibition of discipline is that of the earliest days.

In book iv, ch. 5, enumerating those whose offerings were to be refused by the bishops as unworthy, we have amongst thieves and other sinners.

(Qui) famulos suos dure accipiunt et tractant; id est, verberibus, aut fame afficiunt, aut crudeli servitute premunt.

They who receive and treat their slaves harshly; that is, who whip or famish them, or oppress them with heavy drudgery.

There is no crime in having the slave, but cruelty and oppression are criminal.

In the same book, ch. 11, regards slaves and masters.

De famulis quid amplius dicamus, quam quod servus habeat benevolentiam erga dominum cum timore Dei, quamvis sit impius, quamvis sit improbus, non tamen cum eo religione consentiat. Item dominus servum diligat, et quamvis præstet ei, judicet tamen esse æqualitatem, vel quatenus homo est. Qui autem habet dominum Christianum, salvo dominatu, diligat eum, tum ut dominum, tum ut fidei consortem et ut patrem, non sicut servus ad oculum serviens, sed sicut dominum amans, ut qui sciat mercedem famulatûs sui a Deo sibi solvendam esse. Similiter dominus, qui Christianum famulum habet, salvo famulatu, diligat eum tanquam filium, et tanquam fratrem propter fidei communionem.

What farther, then, can we say of slaves, than that the servant should have benevolence towards his master, with the fear of God, though he should be impious, though wicked; though he should not even agree with him in religion. In like manner, let the master love his slave, and though he is above him, let him judge him to be his equal at least as a human being. But let him who has a Christian master, having regard to his dominion love him both as a master, as a companion in the faith and as a father, not as an eye-servant, but loving his master as one who knows that he will receive the reward of his service to be paid by God. So let the master who has a Christian slave, saving the service, love him as a son and as a brother, on account of the communion of faith.

Ne amaro animo jubeas famulo tuo aut ancillæ eidem Deo confidentibus: ne aliquando gemant adversus te, et irascatur tibi Deus. Et vos servi dominis vestris tanquam Deum repræsentantibus subditi estote cum sedulilate et metu, *tanquam Domino, et non tanquam hominibus.*

Do not command your man-servant nor your woman-servant having confidence in the same God, in the bitterness of your soul; lest they at any time lament against you, and God be angry with you. And you servants be subject to your masters, the representatives of God, with care and fear. As to the Lord and not to men.

In the eighth book, ch. 33, is a constitution of SS. Peter and Paul respecting the days that slaves were to be employed in labor, and those on which they were to rest and to attend to religious duties.

Pope Stephen I, who was the 23d Supreme Pontiff, became head of the church in the year 253, and endeavored, to the best of his ability, to preserve discipline, and, in some letters, to set forth regulations as well as to remedy other evils. In Ep. II, regula. iv.

Accusatores vero et accusationes, quas sæculi leges non recipiunt, et antecessores nostri prohibuerunt, et nos submovemus.

We also reject those accusers and charges which the secular laws do not receive, and which our predecessors have prohibited.

Soon after he specifies:

Accusator autem vestrorum nullus sit servus aut libertus.

Let not your accuser be a slave or a freed person.

Thus, as well in the ancient discipline of the church during the first two centuries, as in the secular tribunals, the testimony of slaves was inadmissible in many cases.

In the year 305, a provincial council was held at Elvira, in the southern part of Spain. The fifth Canon of which is the following:

Si qua domina furore zeli accensa flagris verberaverit ancillam suam, ita ut in tertium diem animam cum cruciatu effundat: eo quod incertum sit, voluntate, an casu occiderit, si voluntate post septem annos; si casu, post quinquennii tempora; acta legitima pænitentia, ad communionem placuit admitti. Quod si infra tempora constituta fuerit infirmata, accipiat communionem.

If any mistress, carried away by great anger, shall have whipped her maid-servant so that she shall within three days die in torture, as it is uncertain whether it may happen by reason of her will or by accident, it is decreed that she may be admitted to communion, having done lawful penance, after seven years, if it happened by her will, if by accident, after five years. But should she get sick within the time prescribed, she may get communion.

We can perceive by this canon that the Spanish ladies, at that period, which was twenty years before the celebration of the council of Nice, had not yet so far yielded to the benign influence of the gospel, and so far restrained their violence of temper as to show due mercy to their female slaves. I doubt much whether the enactment of such a law in our southern states would not call forth against the legislators more indignation from our ladies than they have ever exhibited against their waiting maids.

The canon lxxx, of the same council regarded the prohibition of ordaining emancipated slaves or freedmen unless their guardians were the clergy or the church.

It may, perhaps, be as well to observe, in this place, a beneficial change which had taken place, not only in public opinion, but even in the court, by reason of the influence of the humanizing spirit of Christianity; so that even the Pagan more than once reproved, by his mercy, the professor of a better faith who followed a worse practice.

Theodoret (l. 9, de Græc. cur. aff.) informs us that Plato established the moral and legal innocence of the master who slew his slave. Ulpian, the celebrated Roman jurist (l. 2, de his quæ sunt sui vel alieni jur.) testifies the power which—probably in imitation of the Greeks—the Roman masters had over the lives of their slaves. The well known sentence of Pollio upon the unfortunate slave that broke a chrystal vase at supper,— that he should be cast as food to fish,—and the interference of Augustus, who was a guest at that supper, give a strong exemplification of the tyranny then in many instances indulged. Seneca relates the anecdote in his work (de Clement).

Antonius Pius, as Ulpian relates, issued a constitution about the year 150 restraining this power, and forbidding a master to put his own slave to death, except in those cases where he would be permitted to slay the slave of another. He further states that the cruelty of the Spaniards to their slaves, especially in the province of Bœtica, in which the city of Elvira was, gave occasion to the constitution ; and we have a rescript of Antoninus to Ælius Martianus, the proconsul of Bœtica, in the case of the slave of Julius Sabinus, a Spaniard. In this the right of the masters to their slaves is recognized, but the officer is directed to hear their complaints of cruelty, starvation, and oppressive labor; to protect them, and, if the complaints be founded in truth, not to allow their return to the master ; and to insist on the observance of the constitution.

Caius (in l. 2, ad Cornel. de sicar.) states that the cause should be proved in presence of judges before the master could pronounce his sentence. Spartianus, the biographer, informs us that the Emperor Adrian, who was the immediate predecessor of Antoninus, enacted a law forbidding masters to kill their slaves, unless legally convicted. And Ulpian relates, near the end of the above quoted work, that Adrian placed, during five years, in confinement (relegatio) Umbricia, a lady of noble rank, because, for very slight causes, she treated her female slaves most cruelly. But Constantine the great, about the year 320, enacted that no master should, under penalty due to homicide, put his slave to death, and gave the jurisdiction to the judges ; but if the slave died casually, after necessary chastisement, the master was not accountable to any legal tribunal. (Const. in l. i ; C. Theod. de emendat, servorum.)

It will thus be perceived that, as Christianity made progress, the unnatural severity with which this class of human beings was treated became relaxed, and as the civil law ameliorated their condition, the canon law, by its spiritual efficacy, came in with the aid of religion to secure that the followers of the Saviour should give full force to the merciful provisions that were introduced.

It will also be seen that the principle which St. Augustine laid down was that observed, viz., The state was to enact the laws regulating this species of property; the church was to plead for morality and to exhort to practice mercy.

About the same time, St. Peter, Archbishop of Alexandria, in Egypt, drew up a number of penitential canons, pointing out the manner of receiving, treating and reconciling the " lapsed," or those who through fear of persecution, fell from the profession of the faith. Those canons were held in high repute, and were generally adopted by the eastern bishops. St. Peter succeeded Theonas in that see, in the year 300, and was beheaded by order of the Emperor Maximus, in 311. He ordained Arius, deacon, but subsequently excommunicated him for his pride and his obstinacy.

The sixth of those canons, exhibits to us, a curious device of weak Christians, who desired to escape the trials of martyrdom, without being guilty of actual apostacy. A person of this sort procured, that one of his slaves should personate him, and in his name should apostatize. The canon prescribes for such a slave, who necessarily was a Christian and a slave of a Christian, but one third of the time required of a free person, in a mitigated penance, taking into account the influence of fear of the master, which, though it did not excuse, yet, it diminished the guilt of the apostacy.

The general Council of Nice, in Bythinia, was held in the year 325, when Constantine was emperor. In the first canon of this council, according to the usual Greek and Latin copies, there is a provision for admitting slaves as well as free persons who have been injured by others, to holy orders. In the Arabic copy, the condition is specially expressed, which is not found in the Greek or Latin, but which had been previously well known and universally established, *viz.* that this should not take place unless the slave had been manumitted by his master.

About this period, also, several of the Gnostic and Manichean errors prevailed extensively in Asia Minor. The fanatics denied the lawfulness of marriage; they forbid meat to be eaten; they condemned the use of wine; they praised extravagantly the monastic institutions, and proclaimed the *obligation on all* to enter into religious societies; they decried the lawfulness of slavery; they denounced the slaveholders as violating equally the laws of nature and of religion; they offered to aid slaves to desert their owners; gave them exhortations, invitations, asylum and protection; and in all things assumed to be more holy, more perfect, and more spiritual than other men.

Osius, bishop of Cordova, in Spain, whom Pope Sylvester sent as his legate into the east, and who presided in the Council of Nice, was probably present, when, about the period of the Nicene Council, several bishops assembled in the city of Gangræ, in Paphlagonia, to correct those errors. Pope Symmachus declared in a council held in Rome, about the year 500, that Osius confirmed by the authority of the Pope, the acts of this council. The decrees have been admitted into the body of canon law, and have always been regarded as a rule of conduct in the Catholic church. The third canon is as follows:

Si quis docet servum, pietatis prætextu, dominum contemnere, et a ministerio recedere, et non cum benevolentia et omni honore domino suo inservire. Anathema sit.

If any one, under the pretence of piety, teaches a slave to despise his master, and to withdraw from his service, and not to serve his master with good will and all respect. Let him be Anathema.

This last phrase: *Let him be Anathema,* is never appended to any decree which does not contain the expression of unchangeable doctrine respecting belief or morality, and indicates that the doctrine has been revealed by God. It is precisely what St. Paul says in *Galat.* i, 8. " But though we, or an angel from Heaven, preach a gospel to you beside that which we have preached to you, let him be Anathema." 9. " As we said before to you, so I say now again: If any man preach to you a gospel besides that which you have received; let him be Anathema." It is therefore manifest, that although this Council of Gangræ was a particular one, yet the universal reception of this third canon with its anathema, and its recognition in the Roman Council by Pope Symmachus, gives it the greatest [authority, and in Labbé it is further entitled as approved by Leo IV, about the year 850, *dist. 20, C. de libell.*

Several councils were held in Africa in the third and fourth centuries, especially, in Carthage, in Milevi and in Hippo. About the year 422, which was the first of Pope Celestine I, one was held under Aurelius, Archbishop of Carthage, and in which St. Augustin sat as bishop of Hippo and legate of Numidia. A compilation was made of the canons of this and the preceding ones which I have mentioned, and this was styled the "African Council." The canon cxvi, of this collection, which has also been taken into the body of the canon law, decrees that slaves shall not be admitted as prosecutors, nor shall certain freedmen be so admitted, except to complain for themselves, and for this as well as for the incapacity of several others there described, the public law is cited as well as the 7th and 8th councils of Carthage.

The great St. Basil, Archbishop of Cæsarea in Cappadocia, was born in 329, and died in 379. Amongst his works are his letters, called "Canonical," as they contain a great number of those which were the rules of discipline not only for Asia Minor but for the vast regions in its vicinity. Mentioning marriages, and writing of several cases in which they are lawful or unlawful, valid or invalid, the fortieth canon regards the marriages of female slaves. In this he mentions a discipline which was not general, but was peculiar to the north eastern provinces of the church, requiring the consent of the master to the validity of the marriage contract of a female slave; this was not required in other places, as is abundantly testified by several documents.

The forty-second canon treats in like manner of the marriages of children without their parents' consent, and generally of those of all slaves without the consent of the owner.

The fifty-third canon regards a female slave who has become a widow.

I shall conclude for this day, but shall follow up the documentary evidence for the legality of holding slaves.

I have the honor to be, sir,

Respectfully, &c.

† John, Bishop of Charleston.

Charleston, S. C., *October* 28, 1840.

LETTER VI.

To the Hon. JOHN FORSYTH, Secretary of State, U. S.

Sir,—In my last, I examined the canonical regulations respecting slavery during the four first centuries of Christianity: during the latter of these, the Christians had the government of the civilized world. At this period the barbarous hordes began to pour extensively their desolating masses over the regions in which Arianism was contending with Catholicity. Had peace been granted immediately after the cessation of pagan persecution, and had the church been able to preserve her dominion over all or the greater number that professed the Christian name, it is probable that the mild spirit of religion would have not only improved the condition of the slaves, but would have dissolved the chains by which many of them were bound.

The Arian succeeded the Pagan, and the Goths of various clans soon were found dismembering the ancient empire of the Romans. The Circumcellions of Africa had scarcely disappeared before the Visigoths, when the untamed Attila, with his wild Huns, sweeping along the Danube and the Rhine, carried desolation into Gaul, and disturbed the followers of Pharamond, and the Goths who had lately established themselves in many of the strong holds of the ancient Gauls and more modern Romans. His career was arrested on the banks of the Rhone, as he was rushing towards the Mediterranean. Returning to Pannonia, he recruited his force, and directed his march towards Italy. Aquileia still exhibits, after fourteen centuries, as distinct a monument of the barbarity of the Huns as Mount Benedict does, after six years, of the ruthless and unmanly bigotry of the Bostonians. History attests the extraordinary manner in which, flushed with victory and ambitious of spoils, he, at the monition and request of Pope St. Leo I, turned the tide of his host, and withdrew to his fastnesses beyond the Danube. The captives made on both sides in these desolating incursions, increased the number of slaves, which from other causes had been greatly reduced.

As early as the days of St. Polycarp and St. Ignatius, who were disciples of the apostles, Christians had, from motives of mercy, charity and affection, manumitted many of their slaves in presence of the Bishops, and this was more or less extensively practised through the succeeding period. In several particular churches, it was agreed that if a slave became a Christian, he should be manumitted on receiving baptism. In Rome, the slave was frequently manumitted by the form called *Vindicta*, with the prætor's rod. Constantine, in the year 317, as Sozomen relates, lib. 1, c. 9, transferred this authority to the bishops, who were empowered to use the rod in the church, and have the manumission testified in the presence of the congregation. A rescript of that emperor to this effect is found in the Theodosian code, *l.* 1, *c. de his qui in Eccl. manumitt.* The master, who consented to manumit the slave, presented him to the bishop, in presence of the congregation, and the bishop pronounced him free and became the guardian of his freedom. The rescript was directed to Protogenas, bishop of Sardica, and was in the Consulship of Sabinus and Ruffinus.

In book 2, of the same code, is a rescript to Osius, Bishop of Cordova, in which the emperor empowers the bishops to grant the privilege of Roman citizenship to such freedmen as they may judge worthy.

In the Consulship of Crispus and Constantine, a grant was given to the clergy of manumitting their own slaves when they pleased, by any form they should think proper. About a century later, St. Augustine, Bishop of Hippo, informs us (*Sermo. de diversis,* 50,) that this form was established in Africa. "The deacon of Hippo is a poor man: he has nothing to give to any person: but, before he was a clergyman, he, by the fruit of his labor and industry, bought some little servants, and is to-day, by the episcopal act, about to manumit them in your sight."

This same holy bishop writes (*Enarrat in Psal.* cxxiv.) "Christ does not wish to make you proud whilst you walk in this journey, that is, whilst you are in this life. Has it happened that you have been made a Christian, and you have a man as your master: you have not been made a Christian that you may scorn to serve. When, therefore, by the command of Christ you are the servant of a man, your service is not to him but to the one that gave you the command to serve. And he says: Hear your masters, according to the flesh, with fear and trembling, and in the simplicity of your hearts, not as eye-servants, as if pleasing men, but, as the servants of Christ, doing the will of God, from your hearts, with a good will. Behold, he did not liberate you from being servants, but he made those who were bad servants to be good servants. O, how much do the rich owe to Christ who has thus set order in their houses! So, if there be in his family a faithless slave, and Christ convert him, he does not say to him, 'Leave your master, because you have now known him who is the true master! Perhaps this master of yours is impious and unjust, and that you are faithful and just, it is unbecoming that the just and faithful should serve the unjust and the infidel: this is not what he said; but, let him rather serve." This great Doctor of the Church continues then at considerable length to show how Christ, by his own example, exhorts the servants to fidelity and obedience to their masters in every thing, save what is contrary to God's service. Subsequently, he passes to the end of time, and the opening of eternity, and shows many good, obedient and afflicted servants mingled with good masters among the elect, and bad, faithless and stubborn servants, with cruel masters, cast among the reprobates.

In his *book* i, *on the Sermon of Christ on the mountain,* he dwells upon the duty of Christian masters to their slaves. They are not to regard them as mere property, but to treat them as human beings having immortal souls, for which Christ died.

Thus, we perceive that though from the encouragement of manumission and the spirit of Christianity, the number of slaves had been greatly reduced and their situation greatly improved, still, the principles were recognised, of the moral and religious legality of holding slave property, and of requiring that they should perform a reasonable service.

We have next to consider a canon enacted by that same Leo the great, who caused " the scourge of God," Attila, to spare Italy. Indeed, it is rather the repressing of an abuse, by enforcing an ancient canon. It is found the first of five which he promulgated to the Bishops of Campania and the Picene territory, in the year 445. The instances of voluntary slavery, such as that related of St. Paulinus of Nola, in Campania, were not very rare. It is related by St. Gregory, that having bestowed all that he could raise, to ransom prisoners taken by the barbarians who overran the country; upon the application of a poor widow whose son was held in captivity, he sold himself, to procure the means of her son's release. His good conduct procured the affection of his master, and subsequently his emancipation. Thus slavery lost some of its degrading character. This, together with the confusion arising from the turbulence accompanying the invasions, caused a relaxation of discipline: to remedy some of the abuses, Pope Leo issued several letters. The following is an extract from the first of them: it has been taken into the body of the canon law. *Dist.* 5, *Admittuntur :—*

Admittuntur passim ad ordinem sacrum, quibus nulla natalium, nulla morum dignitas suffragatur: et qui a dominis suis libertatem consequi minime potuerunt, ad fastigium sacerdotii, tanquam servilis vilitas hunc honorem jure capiat, provehuntur: et probari Deo se posse creditur, qui domino suo necdum probare se potuit. Duplex itaque in hac parte reatus est, quod et sacrum mysterium (ministerium) talis consortii vilitate polluitur, et dominorum, quantum ad illicitæ usurpationis temeritatem pertinet, jura solvuntur. Ab his itaque, fratres carissimi, omnes provinciæ vestræ abstineant sacerdotes: et non tantum ab his, sed ab illis etiam, qui

aut originali, aut alicui conditioni obligati sunt, volumus temperari : nisi
forte eorum petitio aut voluntas accesserit, qui aliquid sibi in eos vendicant
potestatis. Debet enim esse immunis ab aliis, qui divinæ militiæ fuerit
aggregandus ; ut a castris Dominicis, quibus nomen ejus adscribitur, nullis
necessitatis vinculis abstrahatur.

*" Persons who have not the qualifications of birth or conduct, are every
where admitted to holy orders ; and they who could not procure freedom
from their masters are elevated to the rank of the priesthood ; as if the lowliness of slavery could rightfully claim this honor : and, as if he who could
not procure the approbation of even his master, could procure that of God.
There is, therefore, in this a double criminality : for the holy ministry is
polluted by the meanness of this fellowship, and so far as regards the rashness of this unlawful usurpation, the rights of the masters are infringed.
Wherefore, dearest brethren, let all the priests of your province keep aloof
from these : and not only from these, but also, we desire they should abstain
from those who are under bond, by origin or any condition, except perchance
upon the petition or consent of the persons who have them in their power in
any way. For he who is to be aggregated to the divine warfare, ought to
be exempt from other obligations : so that he may not by any bond of necessity be drawn away from that camp of the Lord, for which his name has
been enrolled."*

Prosper *lib.* 2, *de vitâ contemplat. c.* 3, and many other writers of this
century, treat of the relative duties of the Christian master and his Christian slave. The zeal and charity of several holy men led them to make
extraordinary sacrifices also, during this period, to redeem the captives
from the barbarians : besides the remarkable instance of St Paulinus, we
have the ardent and persevering charity of St. Exuperius, Bishop of Toulouse, who sold the plate belonging to the church, and used glass for the
chalice, that he might be able by every species of economy to procure
liberty for the enslaved.

The right of the master, the duty of the slave, the lawfulness of continuing the relation, and the benevolence of religion, in mitigating the
sufferings of those in bondage and releasing them by lawful means
permitted by the state, are the results exhibited by our view of the laws
and facts during the four first centuries of Christianity.

It is proper here also to notice, that amongst several of those barbarians,
especially after they embraced the Christian religion, slavery began to
assume a variety of mitigated forms, which will be in some degree develop-
ed as we proceed with the history of canonical legislation.

About the year 494, Pope Gelasius, issued a constitution, in which he
mentions, amongst other monitions given to a bishop at his ordination:

"Ne unquam ordinationes præsumat illicitas; ne * * * * * curæ aut cuilibet conditioni obnoxium, notatumque ad sacros ordines permittat accedere." *That he should never presume to hold unlawful ordinations ; that he should not allow to holy orders, * * * * * any person bound to the service of the court, or liable to bond from his condition* (slavery) *or marked thereto.*

In the year 506, which was the 22d year of Alaric's reign, and the 8th of Pope Symmachus, a council was held at Agdle, in France, in the present department of Herault, which was then under the dominion of the Visigoths who had subjugated Spain. The sixty second canon of which is the following :

"Si quis servum proprium sine conscientiâ judicis occiderit, excommunicatione, vel pœnitentiâ biennii reatum sanguinis emendabit."

If any one shall put his own servant to death, without the knowledge of the judge, let him make compensation for the guilt of blood by excommunication or two years' penance.

Another council was held eleven years later, in the fourth year of Pope Hormisdas and the 6th of King Childibert, to whom Clovis had given a part of his territory after he had slain Alaric in battle. This council was held at Epao or Epanum, which was near the Rhone, it is supposed not far from lake Leman, near Geneva. At this period it was usual to hold ecclesiastical assemblies at a distance from the distraction of the cities, and removed from the influence of petty tyrants, generally in some large country residence. Many of the canons of this Synod of Epao are little more than transcripts of those of Agdle. The 34th, is—

"Si quis servum proprium sine conscientiâ judicis occiderit, excommunicatione biennii effusionem sanguinis expiabit."

If any one shall slay his own servant without the knowledge of the judge, let him expiate the shedding of blood by an excommunication of two years.

Thus we find that at this period, nearly two hundred years after the law of Constantine forbidding this exercise of power by the master ; the practice existed under the Goths, the Gauls and the Franks. Several authors however interpret these enactments as regarding manslaughter or unintentional slaying, because it is generally believed, that at all times, the period was seven years for voluntary homicide.

Several councils were held in the city of Orleans, in the department of Loiret, in France. The third council of Orleans was held in the year 538, the second of Pope Silverius, and 27th of Childebert, king of the Franks.

The thirteenth canon regulates, that if Christian slaves shall be possessed by Jews, and these latter require them to do any thing forbidden by the Christian religion, or if the Jews shall seize upon any of their servants to whip or punish them for those things that have been declared to be excusable or forgiven, and those slaves fly to the church for protection, they are not to be given up, unless there be given and received a just and sufficient sum to warrant their protection.

The canon xxvi, gives us a specimen of the early feudalism nearly similar to the subsequent villain service.

"Ut nullus servilibus colonariisque conditionibus obligatus, juxta statuta sedis Apostolicæ, ad honores ecclesiasticos admittatur; nisi prius aut testamento, aut per tabulas legitime constiterit absolutum. Quod si quis episcoporum, ejus qui ordinatur conditionem sciens, transgredi per ordinationem inhibitam fortasse voluerit, anni spatio missas facere non præsumat."

Let no one held under servile or colonizing conditions be admitted to church honors, in violation of the statutes of the Apostolic see; unless it be evident that he has been previously absolved therefrom by will or by deed. And if any bishop being aware of such condition of the person so ordained, shall wilfully transgress by making such unlawful ordination, let him not presume to celebrate mass for the space of a year.

The colonial condition was in its origin different from the mere servile. The *mancipium* or *manu captum* was the *servus* or slave made in war: the *colonus*, or husbandman, though at the period at which we are arrived, frequently he was in as abject a condition, yet was so by a different process. St. Augustine in cap. i, *lib. x, De Civitate Dei*, tells us, "Coloni *dicuntur*, qui conditionem debebant genitali solo propter agriculturam sub dominio possessorum." They are called *colonists who owe their condition to their native land, under the dominion of its possessors.*

The following history of various modes by which they became servants, is taken from the work *De Gubernat. Dei. lib. 5*, by the good and erudite Salvianus, a priest, who died at Marseilles, about the year 484.

Nonnulli eorum de quibus loquimur, * * * * cum domicilia atque agellos suos pervasionibus perdunt, aut fatigati ab exactoribus deserunt, quia tenere non possunt, fundos majorum expetunt, et coloni divitum fiunt. Aut sicut solent hi qui hostium terrore compulsi, ad castella se conferunt, aut qui perdito ingenuæ incolumitatis statu ad asylum aliquod desperatione confugiunt: ita et isti qui habere amplius vel sedem vel dignitatem suorum natalium non queunt, jugo se inquilinæ abjectionis addicunt: in hanc necessitatem redacti, ut exactores non facultatis tantum, set etiam conditionis suæ, atque exultantes non a rebus tantum suis, sed etiam a seipsis, ac perdentes secum omnia sua, et rerum proprietate careant, et jus liber-

tatis amittant. * * * * * Illud gravius et acerbius, quod additur huic malo servilius malum. Nam suscipiuntur advenæ, fiunt præjudicio.habitationis indigenæ, et quos suscipiunt ut extraneos et alienos, incipiunt habere quasi proprios : quos esse constat ingenuos, vertunt in servos.

Some of those when they lose their dwellings and their little fields invasion, or leave them, being worried by exactions, as they can no longer hold them, seek the grounds of the larger proprietors, and become the colonists of the wealthy. Or, as is usual with those who are driven off by the fear of enemies, take refuge in the castles, or who, having lost their state of safe freedom fly to some asylum in despair: so they who can no longer have the place or the dignity derived from their birth, subject themselves to the abject yoke of the sojourner's lot ; reduced to such necessity, that they are stripped not only of their property but also of their rank, going into exile not only from what belongs to them but from their very selves, and with themselves losing all that they had, they are bereft of any property in things and lose the very right of liberty. * * * *A more degrading injury is added to this evil. For they are received as strangers, they become inhabitants bereft of the rights of inhabitants, they who receive them as eigners and aliens begin to treat them as property, and change into slaves those who, evidently, were free.*

We are not, sir, without a large host of our *Native American Society* who enter very fully into the views of the hospitable proprietors whom Salvian describes.

In this picture of the colonist, we may find the outline of the villain of a later age; and in the several enactments and regulations of succeeding legislators and councils, we shall discover the changes which the features of servitude underwent, previous to its nearly total extinction in Europe.

Flodoardin c. 28 of history of the church of Rheims, gives us the will of St. Remi, its bishop, who baptized Clovis, upon his conversion in 496, and who was still living in the year 550. This document grants freedom to some of the colonists belonging to that church and retains others in service. Critics are divided in opinion as to the document being a correct copy; but it shows, at all events, that at this period the church did not consider it criminal to hold such property.

Du Cange says, (Art. *Colonus*) that though in several instances the condition of the colonists was as abject as that of slaves, yet generally they were in a better position. *Erant igitur coloni mediæ conditionis inter ingenuos seu liberos et servos.*

Very urgent duties will prevent my resuming this historical exhibition for two or three weeks. Meantime, sir, I have the honor to be, respectfully, &c.

† JOHN, *Bishop of Charleston.*

CHARLESTON, S. C., *November 4th,* 1840.

LETTER VII.

To THE HON. JOHN FORSYTH, SECRETARY OF STATE, U. S.

Sir,—I have exhibited an outline of ecclesiastical legislation respecting slaves during more than five centuries of the early period of the Christian Church. I remarked that a variety of circumstances gave new modifications to slavery, and I exhibited one or two instances, of that change in the class of colonists. It will be necessary for me, before proceeding farther, to remark at greater length upon the nature of that variety, in order to understand better the canons which in many instances are found in the subsequent enactments.

When so erudite an antiquarian as Muratori, treating of the Roman slaves and freedmen, acknowledges that he is unable accurately to state the conditions on which they manumitted their slaves, it would be folly for me to undertake the task. In his treatise "SOPRA I SERVIE, LIBERTI ANTIOCHI," he has a passage which I thus translate :

" We know not whether they manumitted upon condition, or, if so, upon what conditions they manumitted formerly those servants who continued thenceforth as freed persons, but elevated to more honorable employments, to serve in the houses of their masters. We do indeed know in the Tit. *de Operis Libertorum,* and in another *de bonis Libertorum* of the Digests, that very many acquired their liberty with the obligation of giving to their masters presents, or doing work if they were artists, *Operas vel donum.* This was in all likelihood practised only by merchants or other masters given to making profit but not by noble houses. As to these the ancient inscriptions exhibit to us that very many who obtained their freedom, yet continued to live and to do service in those same houses, no longer as slaves but as freed persons, because probably each party found it beneficial. The patrons kept about them persons in whom they had confidence and who had already been engrafted on their families ; the freed persons grown to honor and making profit, could create property for themselves and for their children. I cannot discover whether the Romans had hireling servants as is now the case. They then had true slaves and sometimes freed persons. This being the case, it is matter of surprise that Pignoria in treating of the employment of the ancient slaves should have been so perplexed as not to be able clearly to distinguish slaves from freed persons, and should have attributed to the former many employments which were specially reserved for the latter : and it is more to be wondered at, that marbles which speak of freed persons are referred to by him and explained as treating of slaves."

Noi non sappiamo se cun patti, e con quai patti una vulta si manomettessero que' Servi, che poi continuavano come Liberti a servire in Casa de' loro Padroni, con essere alzati a pin onorati impieghi. Sappiamo bensi dal Tit. *ne Operis Libertorum*, e dall' altro *de bonis Libertorum* ne' Digesti, che moltissimi acquistavane la Liberta con obbligarsi di fare ai Padroni de' Regaii, o delle Fatture, se erano Artefici, *Operas, vel Donum*. Questo si praticava verisimilmente dai soli Mercatanti, ed altri Signori dati all' interasse, ma non gia dalle Nobili Case. Per conto di questo, le antiche Iscrizioni ci fanno vedere, che moltissimi furono coloro, che anche dopo la conseguita Liberta seguitavano a convivere, e servire in quelle medesime Case, non piu come Servi, ma come Liberti, perche probabilmente tornava il conto agli uni, e agli altri. I Padroni si servivano di Persone loro confidenti, e gia innestate nella propria Famiglia ; ei Liberti cresciuti di onore, e di guadagno poteano ceumulara roba per se, e per li Figli. Non ho io potuto scoprire se i Romani tenessero Servi Mercenarj come oggidi. O di veri Servi, o di Liberti allora si servivano. Cio posto, maraviglia e, che il Pignoria in trattando degli Ufizj de' Servi antichi, imbrogliasse tanto le carte, senza distinguere i Servi dai Liberti, e con attribuir molti impieghi ai primi, che pure erano riserbati agli ultimi. E piu da stupire e, citarsi da lui Marmi, che parlano di Liberti, e pure sono presi da esso, come se parlassero di Servi.

Thus it is clear that even in the days of the Emperor Claudius, to whose reign, A. D. 45, the marble of which he treats refers, and probably long before that period, many of the freedmen of the Roman empire were bound to do certain services for the patrons who had been their masters, and that this obligation descended to their progeny. Hence this would still be a species of servitude.

The barbarians who overran the empire came chiefly from Scythia and from Germany, as that vast region was then called, which stretches from the Alps to the Northern Ocean. And when they settled in the conquered provinces of Gaul and in Italy itself, they introduced many of their customs and principles as well of government as of policy. Most of their slaves were what the writers of the second, third and fourth centuries describe as *coloni* and *conditionibus obligati*. As Tacitus describes in xxv. *De Moribus Germanorum*, of which the following is Murphy's translation :—

" The slaves in general are not arranged at their several employments in the household affairs, as is the practice at Rome. Each has his separate habitation, and his own establishment to manage. The master considers him as an agrarian dependent, who is obliged to furnish a certain quantity of grain, of cattle, or of wearing apparel. The slave obeys, and the state of servitude extends no further. All domestic affairs are managed by the master's wife and children. To punish a slave with stripes, to load him with chains, or condemn him to hard labor, is unusual. It is true, that slaves are sometimes put to death, not under color of justice, or of any authority vested in the master; but in a transport of passion, in a fit of rage, as is often the case in a sudden affray; but it is also true, that this species of homicide passes with impunity. The freedmen are not of much higher consideration than the actual slaves; they obtain no rank in their master's family, and, if we except the parts of Germany where monarchy is established, they never figure on the stage of public business. In despotic governments they rise above the men of ingenuous birth, and even eclipse the whole body of the nobles. In other states the subordination of the freedmen is a proof of public liberty."

In the appendix to the Theodosian code, *Const. 5*, we read, "Inverecundâ arte defendetur, si hi ad conditionem vel originem reposcuntur, quibus tempore famis, cum in mortem penuria cogerentur, opitulari non potuit Dominus aut patronus."

It is forbidden as a shameless trick; that an effort should be made to regain to their condition or original state, those whom the master or patron could not aid when in a period of famine they were pressed nearly to death by want.

This exhibits the obligation on the patron of the person *under condition*, and on the master of the slave to support them, and the destruction of their title by the neglect of their duty.

Du Cange calls this *condition* "obnoxitatio," which we may perhaps translate *liability*, "tributum" *a tribute*, "pensitatio," which is generally considered to be "*a yearly payment.*"

It will then suffice for my present purpose to have shown, that at this period of the sixth century, there existed unconditional slavery, and a conditional servitude, or that of persons bound either for freedom received, or for other cause, to render personal service or tribute in kind or yearly pension in payment in coin, as also colonists, some of whom were absolute slaves, but attached to the land upon which they wrought, and who owed their whole service to their owners, and other colonists who had the produce of the land, but were bound thereto and obliged to pay certain portions of that produce to the proprietor, but were in all other respects free to act as they thought proper, and to use the fruits of the soil as they thought proper.

Muratori justly observes, that in process of time, the special agreements and particular enactments regarding the *conditions*, gave such a variety as baffled all attempts at classification and precision.

At a much earlier period, slaves had become a drug in the Italian market. When about the year 405, Rhadagasius, the Goth, was leading upwards of three hundred thousand of his barbarians into Italy, the Emperor Honorius ordered the slaves to be armed for the defence of the country, by which arming they generally obtained their freedom : Stilichon, the consul, slew nearly 150,000 of the invaders in the vicinity of Florence, and made prisoners of the remainder, who were sold as slaves at the low price of one piece of gold for each. Numbers of them died within the year, so that Baronius relates, (Annals A. D. 406,) that the purchasers had to pay more for their burial than for their bodies ; according to the remarks of Orosius—In this state of the market, it was easy for the slave to procure that he should be held *at a condition*, and thenceforth the number under condition greatly increased, and in process of time, became more numerous than those in absolute slavery.

This hasty and imperfect view will elucidate much of the phraseology of our legislation. I now proceed to exhibit the action of the councils respecting slavery. In the year 541, some dates would make it appear 545, the fourth council of Orange was celebrated, in the xxxth year of king Childebert. The following is its ninth canon.—" Ut episcopus, qui de facultate propria ecclesiæ nihil relinquit, de ecclesiæ facultate si quid aliter quam canones eloquuntur obligaverit, vendiderit aut distraxerit, ad ecclesiam revocetur, (ab ecclesia, *in other editions*). Sane si de servis ecclesiæ libertos fecit numero competenti, in ingenuitate permaneant, ita ut ab efficio ecclesiæ non recedant."

Be it enacted, *That a bishop who has left none of his private property to the church, shall not dispose of any of the church property, otherwise than as the canons point out. Should he bind or sell or separate anything otherwise, let it be recalled for the church. But if, indeed, he has made freedom o slaves of the church, to a reasonable number, let them continue in their freedom, but with the obligation of not departing from the duty of the church.*

The Canon xxiii, of the same council is—

" Ut servis ecclesiæ, vel sacerdotum, prædas et captivitates exercere non liceat : quia iniquum est, ut quorum domini redemptionis præstare solent suffragium, per servorum excessum, disciplina ecclesiastica maculetur."

That it be not lawful for the slaves of the church, or of the priests, to go on predatory excursions or to make captives, for it is unjust that when the masters are accustomed to aid in redeeming, the discipline of the church should be disgraced by the misconduct of the slaves.

The canon in prohibiting the abuse, not only shows the existence of slavery, but that it was not considered criminal in the church as a corporation, or in the clergyman as an individual, to hold such property. Many of our modern infidel writers, generally styled liberal, have copied and enlarged upon and adduced also as irrefragable witnesses, ancient writers inimical to the church, who have described the incursions of these slaves and dependants in this and subsequent ages; connecting their misdeeds with the church, describing them as instigated by prelates and by priests to commit robberies for the benefit of religion, and concealing studiously from view the efforts made by churchmen, not only to restrain their wickedness, but to protect their victims, and never alluding to the sacrifices made by the clergy to compensate the sufferers.

But that these were not the only abuses, against which the church had to contend in those disastrous times, the next canon will exhibit. In Judaism, God had established a limited sanctuary for slaves and for certain malefactors, not to encourage crime, but to protect against the fury of passion, and to give some sort of aid to the feeble. Paganism adopted the principle, and the Christian temple and its precincts, became not only by common consent, but by legal enactment the sanctuary instead of the former. Like every useful institution, this too was occasionally abused.

The xxixth Canon was—

" Quæcumque mancipia sub specie conjugii ad Ecclesiæ septa confugerint, ut per hoc credant posse fieri conjugium, minime eis licentia tribuatur, nec talis conjunctio a clericis defensetur: quia probatum est, ut sine legitimâ traditione conjuncti, pro religionis ordine, statuto tempore ab Ecclesiæ communione suspendantur, ne in sacris locis turpi concubitu misceantur. De quâ re decernimus, ut parentibus aut propriis dominis, prout ratio poscit personarum, acceptâ fide excusati sub separationis promissione reddantur: post modum tamen parentibus atque dominis libertate concessâ, si eos voluerint propriâ voluntate conjungere."

Let not those slaves who, under pretext of marriage, take refuge within the precincts of the church, imagining that by this they would make a marriage, be allowed to do so, nor let such union be countenanced by the clergy: for it has been regulated that they who form an union, without lawful delivery, should be, for the good order of religion, separated for a fixed period from the communion of the church, so that this vile connexion may be prevented in holy places. Wherefore we decree, that such persons being declared free from the bond of any plighted faith and made to promise a separation, should be restored to their parents or owners as the case may require; to be, however, subsequently, if the parents or owners should grant leave, married with their own free consent.

Thus it would appear, that as we have seen in some parts of the east at an earlier period, now in this portion of the west, the slaves were made incapable of entering into the marriage contract without the owner's consent. This discipline we shall however see, was at a subsequent period very properly abolished : for marriage is one of those natural rights which is not conveyed away by the subjection of the slave.

In this same council, canon xxx, provision is made for affording to the Christians, who are held as slaves by the Jews, not only sanctuary of the church, but in the house of any Christian, until a fair price shall be stipulated for and paid to the Jewish owner, if the Christian be unwilling to return to his service. This is a clear recognization of the right of property in slaves.

Canon xxxi, of this council, provides, that if any Jew shall bring a slave to be a proselyte to his religion, or make a Jew of a Christian slave, or take as his companion a Christian female slave, or induce a slave born of Christian parents to become a Jew under the influence of a promise of emancipation, he shall lose the title to every such slave. And further that if any Christian slave shall become a Jew for the sake of being manumitted *with condition*, and shall continue to be a Jew, the liberty shall be lost and *the condition* shall not avail him.

Canon xxxii, provides that the descendants of a slave wherever they may be, even after a long lapse of time, though there should be neglect, if found upon the land or possession upon which their parents were placed, shall be held to the original conditions established by the deceased proprietor for the deceased parents, and the priest of the place shall aid in enforcing the fulfilment, and any persons, who shall through avarice interpose obstacles, shall be placed under church censures.

The doctrine and discipline of the church of the Franks was like that of other churches in the several regions of Christendom at this period.

A fifth council was held at Orleans, after the death of King Theobert, in the year 549, which was the tenth of Pope Vigilius and the thirty-eighth of King Childebert. The sixth canon of this council relates to the improper ordination of slaves, to which I have previously adverted, and also exhibits to us more distinctly the freedmen *under condition*, classing them in this regard to a certain extent in the same category with slaves.

We also find here reference to a much more ancient canonical regulation, which I do not recollect to have seen elsewhere, punishing the bishop at the will of the owner, for his improper interference with that owner's property, in the slave that he ordained.

CANON VI.—"Ut servum, qui libertatem a dominis propriis non acceperit, aut etiam jam libertum, nullus episcoporum absque ejus tantum voluntate, cujus aut servus est, aut eum absolvisse dignoscitur, clericum audeat ordinare. Quod si quisquam fecerit, si qui ordinatus est a domino revocetur, et ille qui est collator ordinis, si sciens fecisse probatur, sex mensibus missas tantum facere non præsumat. Si vero sæcularium servus esse convincitur, ei qui ordinatus est benedictione servatâ, honestum ordini domino suo impendat obsequium. Quod si sæcularis dominus amplius eum voluerit inclinare, ut sacrò ordini inferre videatur injuriam, duos servos sicut antiqui Canones habent, Episcopus qui eum ordinavit domino sæculari restituat; et episcopus eum quem ordinavit ad ecclesiam suam revocandi habeat potestatem.''

That no bishop shall dare to ordain as a clergyman, the slave who shall not have received licence from his proper owners ; or a person already freed, without the permission of either the person whose servant he is, or of the person who is known to have freed him. And if any one shall do so, let him who is ordained be recalled by his master, and let him who conferred the order, if it be proved that he did so knowing the state of the person, not presume to celebrate mass for six months only.* But if it be proved that he is the servant of lay persons, let the person ordained be kept in his rank and do service for his owner in a way becoming his order ; but if his lay owner debases him under that grade, so as to do any dishonor to his holy order; let the bishop who ordained him give, as the ancient canons enact, two slaves to his master, and be empowered to take him whom he ordained to his church.

The next canon regards manumission, and the protection of those properly liberated from slavery, against the overbearing and injustice of persons who disregarded the legal absolution from service, given even with their own consent, by the authority of the civil government, in the church by the bishop. It more frequently happened that the liberation was made by one and the dragging back to slavery was the act of the heir.

CANON XII.— '' Et quia plurimorum suggestione comperimus, eos qui in Ecclesiis juxta patrioticam consuetudinem a servitio fuerint absoluti, pro libito quorum cumque iterum ad servitium revocari, impium esse tractavimus, ut quod in Ecclesia Dei consideratione a vinculo servitutis absolvitur, irritum habeatur. Ideo pietatis causâ communi consilio placuit observandum, nt quæcumque mancipia, ab ingenuis dominis servitute laxantur, in eâ libertate maneant, quam tunc a dominis perceperunt. Hujusmodi quoque libertas si a quocumque pulsata fuerit, cum justitiâ ab ecclesiis defendatur, præter eas culpas, pro quibus leges collatas servis revocare jusserunt libertates.''

And since we have discovered by information from several, that they who

---

* Canon xxvi, of the first Council of Orange made the suspension ''a year,'' this ''six months only.''

according to the custom of the country were absolved from slavery in the churches, were again at the will of some persons, reduced to slavery; we have regarded it to be an impiety; that what has by a judicial decree* been absolved from servitude in the church of God, should be set at nought. Wherefore, through motives of piety, it is decreed by common counsel, to be henceforth observed; that whatever slaves are freed from servitude by free masters, are to remain in that freedom which they then received from the masters, and should this liberty of theirs be assailed by any person, it shall be defended within the limits of justice by the churches, saving where there are crimes for which the laws have enacted that the liberty granted to servants shall be recalled.

From the above it would appear that the persons then called *liberti*, or freedmen, or the *conditionati* or persons under condition, and probably in some instances, *coloni* or colonists, had slaves, but were not permitted to liberate them, at least without the consent of their own masters, for the canon speaks of only the servants of the *ingenui* or those who enjoyed perfect freedom. We see, also, what is evident from many other sources, that persons who had obtained their freedom, were for some crimes reduced to servitude, and we shall see in future times, even freemen so enslaved for various offences.

Again, in the canon xxii, of this same council, we find provision which exhibits the caution which was used in regulating the right of sanctuary for slaves. This right was, in Christianity, a concession of the civil power, humanely interposing, in times of imperfect security and violent passion, the protecting arm of the church, to arrest the violence of one party so as to secure merciful justice for the other, and to make the compositions of peace and equity be substituted for the vengeance or the exactions of power. It was, so far from being an encouragement to crime, one of the best helps towards civilizing the barbarian.

CANON XXII.—De servis vero, qui pro qualibet culpa ad ecclesiæ septa confugerint, id statuimus observandum, ut, sicut in antiquis constitutionibus tenetur scriptum, pro concessâ culpâ datis a domino sacramentis, quisquis ille fuerit, egrediatur de veniâ jam securus. Enimvero si immemor fidei dominus transcendisse convincitur quod juravit, ut is qui veniam acceperat, probetur postmodum pro eâ cum qualicumque supplicio cruciatus, dominus ille, qui immemor fuit datæ fidei, sit ab omnium communione suspensis. Iterum si servus de promissione veniæ datis sacramentis a domino jam securus exire noluerit, ne sub tali contumacia requirens locum fugæ, domino fortasse disperiat, egredi nolentem a domino eum liceat occupari, ut nullam, quasi pro retentatione servi, quibuslibet modis moles-

---

* *Consideratione*, " By a judicial decree," Du CANGE, *Decretum, Judicium curiæ.*

tiam aut calumniam patiatur ecclesia: fidem tamen dominus, quam pro concessâ veniâ dedit, nullâ temeritate transcendat. Quod si aut gentilis dominus fuerit, aut alterius sectæ, qui a conventu ecclesiæ probatur extraneus, is qui servum repetit personas requirat bonæ fidei Christianas, ut ipsi in personâ domini servo præbant sacramenta: quia ipsi possunt servare quod sacrum est, qui pro transgressione ecclesiasticam metuunt disciplinam.''

We enact this to be observed respecting slaves, who may for any fault fly to the precincts of the church, that as is found written in ancient constitutions, when the master shall pledge his oath to grant pardon to the culprit, whosoever he may be, he shall go out secure of pardon. But, if the master, unmindful of his oath, shall be convicted of having gone beyond what he had sworn, so that it shall be proved that the servant who had received pardon was afterwards tortured with any punishment for that fault, let that master who was forgetful of his oath, be separated from the communion of all. Again, should the servant secured from punishment by the master's oath, be unwilling to go forth, it shall be lawful for the master, that he should not lose the service of a slave seeking sanctuary by such contumacy, to seize upon such a one unwilling to go out, so that the church should not suffer either trouble or calumny by any means on account of retaining such servant: but, let not the master in any way rashly violate the oath that he swore for granting pardon. But, if the master be a Gentile, or of any other sect proved without the church, let the person who claims the slave procure Christian persons of good account who shall swear for the servant's security in the master's name: because they who dread ecclesiastical discipline for transgression can keep that which is sacred.

About this period a council was held at the ancient capital of the Averni, subsequently Auvergne in France, the city was in after times called "Clarus Mons"—now *Clermont*, in *Puy de Dome*. The sixth Canon of this Conc. II, Avernense, is the same in substance and nearly a literal copy of the xxii of Orleans. Aurel. V, enacting the like penalty of six months' suspension from celebrating Mass, against the bishop who in certain cases should ordain a slave.

Thus we find the property in slaves fully recognised by the church in the sixth century.

I have the honor to be, sir,

Respectfully, &c.

† JOHN, *Bishop of Charleston.*

CHARLESTON, S. C., *December 9th*, 1840.

LETTER VIII.

To the Hon. JOHN FORSYTH, Secretary of State, U. S.

Sir,—I shall, for a moment, extend my observations to the most Western part of Europe, known at the period of which I treat, and to a date about one hundred and fifty years prior to that, at which we have arrived.

My object in doing so, is to show, as fully as the evidence within my reach will admit, that the state of those countries, whose ecclesiastical legislation I have produced, differed not, respecting slavery, from the other regions of Europe. The act, to which I am about to refer, is one of those violations of all law and order, of which no one can approve, but a reference to which is absolutely necessary, to understand the history that must be unfolded at a future period of our enquiry.

The Irish had slaves as all the other nations had, and about the year 402, Niell Naoigiallach, or Niel of the Nine Hostages, having ravaged the coast of Britain and Gaul, was slain, in 403, near the Portus Iccius, supposed to be in the vicinity of Boulogne. In this expedition, a large number of captives were made, of whom it is stated, that two hundred were young men of very respectable families: one youth, of only sixteen years of age, by the name of Cothraige, was sold to Milcho, and was employed by him in tending sheep, in a place called Dalradia—within the present county of Antrim. After three years he was delivered, and returned to Gaul, where, some years subsequently, he was reduced again to captivity, by probably a band of roving Franks, but was released after a couple of months. This Cothraige was St. Patrick, subsequently the Apostle of Ireland.

St. Patrick, in his Confessions, states that many of his unfortunate countrymen were carried off and made captives, and dispersed among many nations.

The Romans had possession of Britain, and even had not slavery existed there previously, they would have introduced it; but, unfortunately, the Britons needed not this lesson; they had been abundantly conversant with it before; and, we shall see evidence of the long continuance of its practice.

About the year 450, a party of them, amongst whom were several that professed the Christian religion, made a piratical incursion upon the Irish coast, under the command of Corotic, or Caractacus, which is also sometimes called Coroticus, and which seems to have been in Britain, for a long period, as regular a monarchic appellation as was Pharao in Egypt. Of this incursion, Lanigan compiles the following account, from several authors, to whom he refers, and from whom he quotes in his notes :*

" This prince, Coroticus, though apparently a Christian, was a tyrant, a pirate, and a persecutor. He landed with a party of his armed followers, many of whom were Christians, at a season of solemn baptism, and set about plundering a district (undoubtedly maritime,) in which St. Patrick had just baptized and confirmed a great number of converts, and on the very day after the holy chrism was seen shining in the foreheads of the white-robed neophytes. Having murdered several persons, these marauders carried off a considerable number of people, whom they went about selling or giving up as slaves to the Scots and the apostate Picts. St. Patrick wrote a letter, not extant, which he sent by a holy priest whom he had instructed from his younger days, to those pirates, requesting of them to restore the baptized captives and some part of the booty. The priest and the other ecclesiastics, that accompanied him, being received by them with scorn and mockery, and the letter not attended to, the saint found himself under the necessity of issuing a circular epistle or declaration against them and their chief Coroticus, in which announcing himself a bishop and established in Ireland, he proclaims to all those, who fear God, that said murderers and robbers are excommunicated and estranged from Christ, and that it is not lawful to show them civility, nor to eat or drink with them, nor to receive their offerings, until sincerely repenting they make atonement to God and liberate his servants and the handmaids of Christ. He begs of the faithful, into whose hands the epistle may come, to get it read before the people every where, and before Coroticus himself, and to communicate it to his soldiers, in the hope that they and their master may return to God, &c. Among other very affecting expostulations, he observes, that the Roman and Gallic Christians are wont to send proper persons with great sums of money to the Franks and other Pagans, for the purpose of redeeming Christian captives; while, on the contrary, that monster, Coroticus, made a trade of selling the members of Christ to nations ignorant of God."

The Britons were frequently invaded by the Scots, upon the abandonment of their country by the Romans; and at the period here alluded to, it is supposed by many, that the captives taken from Ireland, were in several instances, given by their possessors to the plundering and victorious Northmen, by the Britons, in exchange for their own captured relatives, whom they desired to release.

Here, sir, we have an instance which will show us the nature of that

---

* NOTE.—Ecclesiastical History of Ireland, Vol. I, chap. iv, § x.

traffic in slaves, which the letter of his Holiness Pope Gregory XVI, condemns, and which was condemned by the legate of Pope Leo the Great, in Ireland, nearly fourteen centuries ago, about the very period when Leo himself turned the fierce Hun Attila, "the scourge of God," from the devastation of Italy, and it was somewhat about this period, that the harassed Britons called, through Vortigern, upon the Saxons Hengist and Horsa, to protect them from their ferocious neighbors on the North. This, sir, will suffice to show us, that not a spot in the then known regions of the globe, could be pointed out, that was exempt from the prevalence of slavery.

I now return to examine the history of ecclesiastical legislation on this subject, during the period subsequent to my last notice. I shall, however, supply an omission that I made in the proceedings of the Council of Clermont, as given in my last, *viz.* that the seventh Canon adopted the principle and enacted the regulations of the 24th Canon of the fourth Council of Orleans, respecting the duty of the bishop to defend the freedom of those who were manumitted. I have also to correct some mistakes of name in that letter, where I gave the appellation of *Orange* to *Orleans*, and did not observe it until too late for correction.

About the year 555, which was the third of Pope Pelagius I, and forty sixth of King Childebert, the third council of Paris was celebrated. In this we find a Canon which is styled *De servis degeneribus*, which in the phraseology of that age, means *bastard servants.—See Du Cange.*

CANON IX.—De degeneribus servis, qui pro sepulchris defunctorum pro qualitate ipsius ministerii deputantur, hoc placuit observari, ut sub quâ ab auctoribus fuerint conditione dimissi, sive heredibus, sive Ecclesiis pro defensione fuerint deputati, voluntas defuncti circa eos in omnibus debeat observari. Quod si Ecclesia eos de fisci functionibus in omni parte defenderit Ecclesiæ tam illi, quam posteri eorum, defensione in omnibus potiantur, et occursum impendant.

It is enacted concerning bastard slaves who are placed to keep the sepulchres, because of the rank of that office, that whether they be placed under the protection of the heirs or of the church for their defence, upon the condition upon which they were discharged by their owners, the will of the deceased should be observed in all things in their regard. But, if the church shall keep them entirely exempt from the services and payments of the fisc, let them and their descendants enjoy the protection of the church for defence and pay to it their tribute.*

The *Auctores* or authors, in the original sense, was *owners* or *masters;* and subsequently, especially in Gaul, it was often taken to mean *parents,*

---

* Note.—*Occursum,* in the style of that age and country, is *tribute* or *payment.*

which probably, from the context, is here its meaning; and, we find a new title and a new class, where the master having committed a crime with his servant, the offspring was his slave; yet, his natural affection caused the parent to grant him a conditioned freedom to protect which this canon specified the guardian to be either the heir or the church.

In or about the year 610, or the second year of king Ariamir, the second Council of Alicant, in the province of Valentia, in Spain, was celebrated: it is styled LUCENSE. II. It received and adopted the *Capitula* or heads of Canons sent to a previous council, Lucense. I. or first of Alicant which was celebrated in the year 607, in the reign of Theodomir, father of Ariamir. These little chapters or heads were transmitted by Martin, archbishop or metropolitan of Braga, who presided at the third Council of that city, in the year 572.

Martin collected from the councils of the east and the west, the greater portion of the canon law then in force and made a compendium thereof, which he distributed into 84 heads which formed as many short canons, and thenceforth they were the basis of the discipline in Spain.

The forty-sixth of these canons is the following—

" Si quis obligatus tributo servili, vel aliqua conditione, vel patrocinio cujuslibet domûs, non est ordinandus clericus, nisi probandœ vitæ fuerit et patroni concessus accesserit."

If any one is bound to servile tribute, or by any condition, or by the patronage of any house, he is not to be ordained a clergyman, unless he be of approved life and the consent of the patron be also given.

This canon is taken into the body of the canon law. *Dist.* 53.

CANON 47.—" Si quis servum alienum causâ religionis doceat contemnere dominum suum et recedere à servitio ejus, durissimè ab omnibus arguatur."

If any person will teach the servant of another under pretext of religion to despise his master and to withdraw from his service, let him be most sharply rebuked by all.

This too is taken into the body of the canon law. (17. q. 4, *Si quis.*) I before observed that this was one of the earliest enactments at Ancyra, in the eastern division of the church, against the fanatics of the third and fourth centuries. Their spirit seems to have transmigrated to our continent and to have animated several of our over-seeming pious folk of the present day.

In the year 589 the third council of Toledo, in Spain, was celebrated, in the pontificate of Pope Pelagius II. All the bishops of Spain assembled upon the invitation of King Recared, and the Goths, after upwards of two centuries of adherence to the Arian heresy, were induced to abandon it and to submit to the church. The articles of Faith form 23 heads of various length; after which follow 23 *Capitula* or little chapters or heads of discipline.

The sixth of these is in the following words :—

VI.—" De libertis autem id Dei prœcepiunt sacerdotes, ut si qui ab episcopis facti sunt secundum modum quo canones antiqui dant licentiam, sint liberi ; et tamen a patrocinio ecclesiæ tam ipsi, quam ab eis progeniti non recedant. Ab aliis quoque libertati traditi, et ecclesiis commendati, patrocinio episcopali regantur : à principe hoc episcopus postulet.''

The priests of God decree concerning freedmen, that if any are made by the bishops in the way the ancient canons permit, they shall be considered free ; yet so that neither they nor their descendants shall retire from the patronage of the church. Let those freed by others and placed under the protection of the church be placed under the bishop's protection. Let the bishop ask this of his prince.

This *commendatio* was a guardianship. The custom was generally to make the church the guardian of those who were emancipated from servitude, yet the freedman owed to his patron or guardian not only great respect but some little service or gift, in return for the protection he received.

The bishops about this period, in many places, were judges, to a certain extent, in those cases where their clergy or others under their charge or belonging to the church were concerned ; but this not by divine right, nor by ecclesiastical authority, but by the concession and commission of the civil power. And this canon or chapter very regularly, when enacting that the bishop as patron should govern such clients or freed persons, refers to the proper source, by adding the expression, " Let the bishop ask his prince"—because the power of temporal rule is in the state not in the church, but when granted to the church by the state, it necessarily was not only validly but legally and properly used.

This too is taken into the body of the canon law—(12. q. 2. *de libertis.*)

A custom had already gained considerable prevalence, which we shall find greatly extended in subsequent ages, of granting to the churches slaves for its service and support. The administrators of the church property were called *familia fisci*. The church property was in ecclesiastical documents generally styled the *fisc*. The *fisca regis* or Royal fisc was a different fund or treasury. It sometimes happened that the clergy who were the administrators sought to obtain from the "conditioned slaves" more than they were bound to give, and also, sometimes, others sought to have their service taken from the church. The Capitulary VIII of this third council of Toledo was enacted to remedy this latter grievance.

" Innuente (other copies Jubente) atque consentiente domino piïssimo

Reccaredo rege, id præcipit sacerdotale consilium, ut clericorum (others, clericos) ex familiâ fisci nullus audeat, a principe donatos expetere; sed reddito capitis sui tributo ecclesiæ Dei, cui sunt alligati, usque dum vivent, regulariter administrent."

By the suggestion (or by the command) and with the consent of the most pious Lord king Reccared, the council of priests directs that no one shall dare to reclaim from the administrators of the church those clergy given by the prince, but having paid their tribute to the church of God, to which they are bound, let them, as long as they live, administer regularly.

In the same council, the Canon XV is the following:

" Si qui ex servis fiscalibus ecclesias forte construxerint easque de suâ paupertate ditaverint, hoc procuret episcopus prece suâ auctoritate regiâ confirmari."

If any of the king's special servants shall have built churches and have enriched them by the contributions from their poverty, let the bishop obtain that it be confirmed by the royal authority.

The *servi fiscales* were the private or patrimonial property of the king, and Binius and Garcia remark that in this canon the *fiscus* means the royal patrimony, as is plain from the edict of the king by which he embodied the temporal enactments found in those canons into the body of the Spanish law, and also enacted fines to his treasury, or confiscation for the violation of any of the decrees of the council.

This also exhibits the principle that the slave was not permitted to contribute, without the consent of his owner, to religious establishments, and in several instances, and as a general principle, nothing could be more wise and just.

I shall conclude my observations for the present, by producing a canon from that collection which is styled that of *Quinisextum*, or the assembly held in 692 in Constantinople, in the hall of the palace called Trulla, whence it is called *Concilium Trullanum* or the Council of Trullo. Some of the acts of this assembly were set aside by the church as exceedingly irregular and of no force, but, other canons, exhibited as theirs, are in perfect conformity with the doctrine and discipline of the Universal Church and generally received as known and admitted rules of discipline. The following is one not only unobjected to, but conformable to what was the general usage. I have before me the Greek original and a Latin accurate translation. I cannot so conveniently have the former printed and shall, therefore, give the latter.

Canon lxxxv.—"In duobus vel tribus testibus confirmari omne verbum ex scriptura accepimus. Servos ergo qui a dominis suis manumittuntur, sub tribus testibus eo frui honore decernimus, qui præsentes libertati vires et firmitatem afferent et ut iis quæ ipsis testibus facta sunt, fides habeatur efficient."

We have learned from the Scripture that every word is confirmed in two or three witnesses. We therefore decree that slaves who are manumitted by their masters shall be admitted to enjoy that honor under three witnesses, who may be able to afford security by their presence to the freedom, and who may be able to secure credit for the acts done in their view.

Thus we have at this period, the legislation respecting slavery in all the portions of the church from the Ganges to the Atlantic, and from Scythia to Ethiopia. We find in Ireland piracy and robbery, and the reducing of freemen by violence in a time of peace by private marauders, and carrying them into bondage into remote countries, condemned by excommunication; but we find domestic slavery of every grade tolerated, and we find slaves to be property of the church.

I shall, I hope, be able to continue without interruption, to follow up my evidence. I have the honor to be, sir,

Respectfully, &c.

† JOHN, *Bishop of Charleston.*

CHARLESTON, S. C., *December* 17, 1840.

LETTER IX.

To THE HON. JOHN FORSYTH, SECRETARY OF STATE, U. S.

SIR,—Perhaps it would be as well that I should give, at length, the following passage from the venerable Bede (Hist. Ecclesiast. Gent. Anglor. Lib. ii, c. 1.) It will at least show the readers of these letters a little morsel of that punning, which was fashionable in the decline of the Roman power, even amongst the best scholars and the most holy men:—

" Nec silentio prætereunda opinio quæ de beato Gregorio, traditione majorum ad nos usque perlata est: quâ videlicet ex causâ admonitus, tam sedulam erga salutem nostræ gentis curam gesserit. Dicunt, quia die quâdam cum advenientibus nuper mercatoribus multa venalia in forum fuissent conlata, multique ad emendum confluxissent, et ipsum Gregorium inter alios advenisse, ac vidisse inter alia pueros venales positos, candidi corporis ac venusti vultus, capillorum quoque formâ egregiâ. Quos cum aspiceret, interrogavit, ut ajunt, de quâ regione vel terrâ essent adlati. Dictumque est quod de Brittaniâ insulâ, cujus incolæ talis essent aspectûs.

Rursus interrogavit, utrum iidem insulani, Christiani, an paganis adhuc erroribus essent implicati. Dictumque est, quod essent pagani. At ille intimo ex corde longa trahens suspiria: "Heu, proh dolor! inquit, quod tam lucidi vultûs homines, tenebrarum auctor possidet, tantaque gratia frontispicii mentem ab internâ gratiâ vacuam gestat !" Rursus ergo interrogavit, quod esset vocabulum gentis illius. Responsum est quod Angli vocarentur. At ille, " Benè, inquit: nam et angelicam habent faciem, et tales angelorum in cœlis decet esse coheredes. Quod habet nomen ipsa provincia de quâ isti sunt adlati ?" Responsum est quod Deiri vocarentur iidem provinciales. At ille: " Benê, inquit, Deiri, de irâ eruti, et ad misericordiam Christi vocati. Rex provinciæ illius quomodo appellatur ?" Responsum est quod *Aella* diceretur. At ille adludens ad nomen ait: " *Alleluia*, laudem Dei creatoris illis in partibus oportet cantari." Accedensque ad Pontificem Romanæ et Apostolicæ sedis, nondum enim erat ipse Pontifex factus, rogavit, ut genti Angliorum in Britanniam aliquos verbi ministros, per quos ad Christum converterentur, mitteret : seipsum paratum esse in hoc opus Domino co-operante perficiendum, si tamen Apostolico Papæ hoc ut fieret, placeret. Quod dum perficere non posset ; quia etsi pontifex concedere illi quod petierat voluit, non tamen cives Romani, ut tam longe ab urbe recederet potuere permittere ; mox ut ipse Pontificatûs officio functus est, perficit opus diu desideratum : alios, quidem Prædicatores mittens, sed ipse Prædicationem ut fructificaret suis exhortationibus et precibus adjuvans."

Nor is that notice of the blessed Gregory which has come down to us by the tradition of our ancestors to be silently passed over : for by reason of the admonition that he then received, he became so industrious for the salvation of our nation. For they say, that on a certain day when merchants had newly arrived, many things were brought into the market and several persons had come to purchase ; Gregory himself came amongst them, and saw exposed for sale, youths of a fair body and handsome countenance, whose hair was also beautiful. Looking at them, they say, he asked from what part of the world they were brought ; he was told from the island of Britain, whose inhabitants were of that complexion. Again he asked whether these islanders were Christians or were immersed in the errors of paganism. It was said : that they were pagans. And he sighing deeply, said ' Alas ! what a pity that the author of darkness should possess men of so bright a countenance, and that so graceful an aspect should have a mind void of grace within !' Again he enquired what was the name of their nation. He was told that they were called Angles. He said, ' It is well, for they have angelic faces, and it is fit that such should be the coheirs with

Angels in Heaven.' *From what province were they brought, was his next enquiry. To which it was answered: The people of their province are* called Deiri. *' Good again,' said he, ' Deiri, (de irâ eruti) rescued from anger and called to the mercy of Christ.'* *What is the name of the king of that province?* He was told Aella. *And playing upon the word he responded ' Alleluia.' The praises of God our Creator ought to be chaunted in those regions. And going to the Pontiff of the Roman Apostolic See, for he was not yet made Pope himself, he besought him to send to Britain for the nation of the Angles, some ministers of the word through whom they may be converted to Christ ; and stated that he was himself ready, the Lord being his aid, to undertake this work, if the Pope should so please. This he was not able to do, for though the Pontiff desired to grant his petition, the citizens of Rome would not consent that he should go to so great distance therefrom ; as soon however as he was placed in the office of Pope, he performed his long desired work, he sent other preachers, but he aided by his prayers and exhortations that he might make their preaching fruitful.*

This occurred about the year 577, and Gregory became Pope in 590. In the interim, the zealous monk prayed and reflected on the subject, and we find that soon after his elevation to the Pontifical dignity, he sought to purchase some of the British youths, in order to have them trained up to be missionaries to their countrymen.

The holy see had already a considerable patrimony in Gaul, bestowed by the piety of the faithful ; we shall see from the following epistle of the Pope to the priest Candidus, whom he sent as its administrator, the use which was made of its income.

Lib. v, *Epist.* x.—Gregorius Candido Presbytero eunti ad patrimonium Galliæ.

"Pergens auxiliante Domino Deo nostro Jesu Christo ad patrimonium, quod est in Galliis gubernandum, volumus ut dilectio tua ex solidis quos acceperit, vestimenta pauperum, vel pueros Anglos, qui sunt ab annis decem et septem, vel decem et octo, ut in monasteriis dati Deo proficiant, comparet ; quatenus solidi Galliarum, qui in terrâ nostrâ expendi non possunt, apud locum proprium utiliter expendantur. Si quid vero de pecuniis redituum, quæ dicuntur ablatæ, recipere potueris, ex his quoque vestimenta pauperum comparare te volumus ; vel, sicut præfati sumus, pueros qui in omnipotentis Dei servitio proficiant. Sed quia pagani sunt, qui illic inveniri possunt, volo, ut cum eis presbyter transmittatur, ne quid ægritudinis contingat in viâ, ut quos morituros conspexerit, debeat baptizare Ita igitur tua dilectio faciat, ut hæc diligenter implere festinet."

GREGORY *to the Priest Candidus going to the patrimony of Gaul.*

As you are going, with aid of the Lord Jesus Christ, our God, to govern the patrimony which is in Gaul; we desire that out of the shillings you may receive, you, our beloved, should purchase clothing for the poor, or English youths about the age of seventeen or eighteen, that being placed in monasteries they may be useful for the service of God ; so that the money of Gaul, which ought not to be expended in our land, may be laid out in its own place beneficially. If you can also get any of the money of that income called tolls, (ablatæ) we also desire that you should therewith buy clothing for the poor, or as we have before said, youths who may become proficients in the service of God. But as they who dwell in that place are pagans, it is our desire that a priest be sent with them lest they should get sick on the journey, and he ought to baptize those whom he may see in a dying state. So let you, our beloved do, and be alert in fulfilling what we have desired.

The commission of Pope Gregory the Great to Candidus was to purchase those youths, and, as we learn from other sources, it was executed. But as Lingard observes, (Ant. Anglo. Saxon Chu. c. i,) "their progress was slow; and his zeal impatient." The result was that St. Augustine and his companions were sent by the Pope, and effected the conversion of the island.

In the same chapter, Lingard describes the Saxons who had settled in England, previous to their conversion, and for that portion which I quote, he refers amongst others to Will. of Malmesbury (*de reg. l. i, c.* 3,) and the testimony is well sustained by others.

" The savages of Africa may traffic with the Europeans for the negroes whom they have seized by treachery, or captured in open war ; but the most savage conquerors of the Britons sold without scruple, to the merchants of the continent, their countrymen, and even their own children."

Nor was slavery abolished by the introduction of Christianity, but its rigors were greatly mitigated. Lingard, in the next page (31) informs us—

" But their ferocity soon yielded to the exertions of the missionaries, and the harsher features of their origin were insensibly softened under the mild influence of the Gospel. In the rage of victory they learned to respect the rights of humanity. Death or slavery was no longer the fate of the conquered Britons ; by their submission, they were incorporated with the victors ; and their lives and property were protected by the equity of their Christian conquerors. * * * * The humane idea, that by baptism, all men become brethren, contributed to meliorate the condition of slavery, and scattered the seeds of that liberality, which gradually undermined, and at length abolished so odious an institution. By the provision of the legislature, the freedom of the child was secured from the avarice of an unnatural parent; and the heaviest punishment was denounced against the man, who presumed to sell to a foreign master one of his countrymen, though he were a slave or a malefactor."

Doctor Lingard refers to the laws of Ina 23, 24, 32, 46, as they are found in Wilkins. I cannot have reference myself to these laws. I had some time since, a copy in my library, of which some one thought proper to deprive me. Nor can I find a copy in this city, but I have no doubt whatever of Lingard's correctness. Ina did not ascend the throne until the year 688, and it was in the fifth year of his reign that he assembled the Witna—gemot, or parliament, in which those laws were enacted. We shall henceforth, have under our eye the legislation on the subject of slavery in England, and shall find that upwards of five hundred years more elapsed before slavery approached the term of abolition in that island.

We have seen Pope St. Gregory the Great purchasing slaves in order to have them educated and ordained; and unless I should show from his works that he regarded and taught the compatibility of slaveholding with the practice of religion, this may be urged as an evidence of abolitionism and of the incompatibility of slavery with his notions of justice. I shall therefore produce evidence to this effect.

In his book "Pastoralis Curæ" *Of the Pastoral care,* part 3, c. i, Admonit. vi, is the following :—

Admonitio VI.—"Aliter admonendi sunt servi, atque aliter domini. Servi scilicet, ut in se semper humilitatem conditionis aspiciant: domini vero, ut naturæ suæ quâ æqualiter sunt cum servis conditi, memoriam non amittant. Servi admonendi sunt ne dominos despiciant, ne Deum offendant si ordinationi illius superbiendo contradicunt: domini quoque admonendi sunt, quia contra Deum de munere ejus superbiunt, si eos quos per conditionem tenent subditos, æquales sibi per naturæ consortium non agnoscunt. Isti admonendi sunt ut sciant se servos esse dominorum: illi admonendi sunt ut cognoscant se conservos esse servorum. Istis namque dicitur: *Servi, obedite dominis carnalibus.* Et rursum: *Quicumque sunt sub jugo servi, dominos suos omni honore dignos arbitrentur:* illis autem dicitur : *et vos, domini, eadem facite illis, remittentes minas, scientes quod et illorum et vester dominus est in cœlis.*"

Admonition VI.—*Servants are to be admonished in one way, masters in another way. Servants indeed that they should always regard in themselves the lowliness of their condition : masters however, that they lose not the recollection of their nature by which they are created upon a level with their slaves; slaves are to be admonished not to despise their masters, lest they offend God, if growing proud they contradict his ordinance: masters too are to be admonished; because they grow proud against God by reason of his gift, if they do not acknowledge as their equals, by the fellowship of nature, those whom by condition they hold as subjects.* These are to be admonished that they be mindful that they are the slaves of their masters: those that they recollect that they are the fellow servants of servants. To these it is said: Servants, obey your masters in the flesh, and again, Whosoever are servants under the yoke: let them consider their masters worthy of all honor: *but to those it is said;* And you masters do in like manner to them: laying aside threats: knowing that your and their master is in heaven.

In his book II, of Epistles, Ep. xxxix, writing to Peter, a subdeacon of Campania, he directs him how to act in the case of a female slave belonging to a proctor or manager of church property, *(defensor)* who was anxious to be allowed to become a sister in a monastery, which was not lawful without the consent of her owner. The Pope neither orders the master to manumit her nor to permit her profession, for though he was employed by the Church, the religion to which he belonged did not require of him to give away his property, nor had the head of that church power to deprive him thereof; hence he writes:—

"Preterea quia Felix defensor puellam nomine Catillam habere dicitur, quæ cum magnis lacrymis, et vehementi desiderio habitum conversionis appetit, sed eam præfatus dominus suus converti minime permittit: proinde volumus, ut experientia tua præfatum Felicem adeat, atque puellæ ejusdem animum sollicitè requirat ; et si ita esse cognoverit, pretium ejusdem puellæ suæ domino præbeat, et huc eam in monasterio dandam cum personis gravibus, Domino auxiliante, transmittat. Ita verò hæc age, ut non per lentam actionem tuam proefatœ puellæ anima detrimentum aliquod in desiderio suo sustineat."

Moreover, because the proctor Felix is said to have a servant named Catilla, who with many tears and vehement desire wishes to obtain the habit of religion; but her aforesaid master will not by any means permit her making profession: it is then our desire that your experience would call upon the said Felix, and carefully examine the disposition of that young woman, and if you should find it such as is stated, pay to the master her price and send her hither with discreet persons to be placed, with God's help, in a monastery. But do this, so that the soul of the young woman may not suffer any inconvenience in her desire, through your tardiness.

The following is a deed of gift which the same Pope made, to assure the possession of a slave to the Bishop of Porto, one of the suburban sees near Rome. It is curious, not merely as exhibiting the fact that the Pope and the See of Rome held and transferred slaves at this period, but also as giving a specimen of a legal document of that date and tenor :—

LIB. X, Ep. LII.—GREGORIUS, Felici Episcopo Portuensi.

"CHARITATIS vestræ gratiâ provocati, ne infructuosi vobis videamur existere, præcipuè cum et minus vos habere servitia noverimus ; ideo Joannem juris Ecclesiastici famulum, natione Sabinum, ex massâ Flavianâ, annorum plus minus decem et octo, quem nostra voluntate jam diu possidetis, fraternitati vestræ jure directo donamus atque concedimus ; ita ut cum habeatis, possideatis, atque juri proprietatique vestra vindicetis atque defendatis, et quidquid de eo facere volueritis, quippe ut dominus, ex hujus donationis jure libero potiamini arbitrio. Contra quam munificentiæ nostræ Chartulam nunquam nos successoresque nostros noveris esse venturos. Hanc autem donationem a Notario nostro perscriptam legimus, atque subscripsimus, tribuentes etiam non expectatâ professione vestrâ quo volueritis tempore alligandi licentiam legitimâ stipulatione et sponsione interpositâ. Actum Romæ."

Excited by our regard for your charitable person, that we may not appear to be useless to you, especially as we know you are short of servants : we therefore give and grant to you our brother, by our direct right, John, a servant of the church domain, by birth a Sabine, of the Flavian property, now aged about eighteen years, whom by our will you have a good while had in your possession. So that you may have and possess him, and preserve and maintain your right to him and defend him as your property. And that you may, by the free right of this donation, enjoy the exercise of your will, to do what you may think proper in his regard, as his lord.

Against which paper of our munificence, you may know that neither we nor our successors are ever to come. And we have read this deed of gift, written out by our Notary, and we have subscribed the same, not even awaiting your profession, respecting the time you would desire license to register it in the public acts by interposing the lawful process of signature and covenant. Done at Rome, &c.

The *Massa* was generally a portion of land : and the servants belonging specially thereto are in the documents of this and a later period generally called either *servi de* (or *ex*) *massa*, and when they subsequently became *conditioned*, or freed to a certain extent, they were called *homines de Masnada* or other names equivalent thereto.

I shall reserve to my next, a form of manumission by which this Pope liberated two slaves.

I shall conclude for this day by giving the following document respecting the release of captives.

LIB. v, Ep. xxxiv.—GREGORIUS, Anthemio Subdiacono :—

" Quantus dolor, quantaque sit nostro cordi afflictio de his, quæ in partibus Campaniæ contigerunt, dicere non possumus : sed ex calamitatis magnitudine potes ipse cognoscere. Eâ de re, pro remedio captivorum qui tenti sunt, solidos experientiæ tuæ per horum portitorem Stephanum virum magnificum transmisimus, admonentes ut omnino debeas esse sollicitus, ac strenuè peragas, et liberos hommes, quos ad redemptionem suam sufficere non posse cognoscis, tu eos festines redimere. Qui vero servi fuerint, et dominos eorum itâ pauperes esse compereris, ut eos redimere non assurgant, et hos quoque comparare non desinas. Pariter etiam et servos Ecclesiæ qui tuâ negligentiâ perierunt, curabis redimere. Quo cumque autem redemeris, subtiliter notitiam, quæ nomina eorum vel quis ubi maneat, sive quid agat, seu unde sit, contineat, facere modis omnibus studebis, quam tecum possis afferre cum veneris. Ita autem in hâc re te studiosè exhibere festina, ut ii qui redimendi sunt, nullum te negligente periculum possint incurrere, et tu apud nos postea vehementer incipias esse culpabilis, sed et hoc quam maxime age, ut si fieri potest, captivos ipsos minori possis pretio comparare. Substantiam verò sub omni puritate atque subtilitate describe, et ipsam nobis descriptionem cum celeritate transmitte."

GREGORY, *to the Subdeacon Anthemius.*

" We cannot express how great is our grief and the affliction of our heart, by reason of what has occurred in a part of Campania ; but you may yourself estimate it from the extent of the calamity. Wherefore we send to your experience, by Stephen, a worthy man, the bearer hereof, money for the aid of those captives, who are detained ; admonishing you that you ought to be very industrious and exert yourself to discover what freemen are unable to procure their own release, and that you should quickly redeem them. But respecting the slaves, when you shall discover that their masters are so poor as not to have it in their power to release them. You will also not omit to buy them. In like manner you will be careful to redeem the servants of the church who have been lost through your neglect.

" You will also be very careful by all means to make a neat brief, which you can bring when you come containing their names, as also where any one remains, how he is employed, or whence he is. You will be diligent and so industrious in this transaction as to give no cause of danger by your neglect for those who are to be released, nor run the risk of being exceedingly culpable in our view. You will be most particular, above all things, to procure the release of the captives at the lowest possible rate. You will make out the accounts as accurately and as clearly as possible, and send them to us with speed."

The calamity which he bewails was an incursion of the Lombards, who coming originally from Scandanavia, settled for a while in Pomerania and about this period ravaged Italy.

We perceive in this epistle the redemption of the freemen, that of slaves whose masters were too poor to pay their ransom, and who were restored by the Pope to their owners, and we find the slaves belonging to the church. Thus we have as much evidence as we need desire, for the compatibility of domestic slavery with true religion at this period.

I shall in my next produce still further evidence from the writings of this excellent witness, Pope St. Gregory the Great, in whose honor the present Pontiff chose the name that he so worthily bears.

I have the honor to be, sir,

Respectfully, &c.

† John, *Bishop of Charleston.*

Charleston, S. C., *December* 22, 1840.

LETTER X.

To the Hon JOHN FORSYTH, Secretary of State, U. S.

Sir,—Before I proceed farther, it may be useful, if not necessary, to advert to the laws of the Roman empire respecting Jews and Christians, and also respecting pagans and Christians, and several of the early sects and Catholics, so far as they regarded slavery. But as the basis of the law should be known, that we may properly learn its nature, it is fit that we should consider how the slave was treated.

The Jew and the Christian were unfortunately in opposition from the very origin of Christianity. The first persecutors of the Christians were the relatives of the first Christians ; the death of the Saviour and the martyrdom of Stephen, the imprisonment of Peter, the mission of Saul to Damascus, and a variety of other similar facts, exhibit to us in strong relief the unfortunate spirit of hatred which caused not merely separation, but enmity. The destruction of Jerusalem, the captivity of the once loved people who preserved the early records of revelation, and the increase of the Christian religion, even under the swords and the gibbets of its persecutors, only increased and perpetuated this feeling.

The pride of the gentile ridiculed what he denominated superstition: whilst he smote the believer whom he mocked, he bowed before the idol of paganism. The early heresies of those who professed the Christian name, but separated from Christian unity, sprung generally from the efforts to destroy the mysterious nature of the doctrine of the apostles, and to explain it by the system of some gentile philosopher, such as Manes or Plato, or to modify it by superinducing some Judaic rite or principle. The Jew, the gentile, and the heretic equally felt elevated by his imagined superiority over the faithful follower of the doctrine of the Galilean, as the Saviour was called. Thus the sword of the persecutor, the scoff of ridicule, and the quibbling of a false philosophy, were all employed against the members of the universal church; and amongst those who were by their situation the most exposed to suffering, were the unfortunate Christian slaves of the enemies of the cross. Even they who belonged to the faithful had peculiar trials, because frequently in times of persecution masters desirous of obtaining protection, without actually sacrificing to idols, compelled their servants to personate them in perpetrating the crime, as is evident from many documents. I may name one, Can. v, of Peter of Alexandria—Τοῖς δὲ δ8λοις.

They were frequently circumcised, even against their will, by the Jewish owners. Can. ii, of Nice I (Arab. 84), "Si quem servorum circumciderunt."

They were frequently mutilated by the infidel master. *Ibid.* They were also exposed to the continued hardships and enticements of owners who desired to make them proselytes, as may be seen in various records.

It was therefore, at an early period after the conversion of Constantine, enacted that no one who was not a Christian should hold a Christian slave, upon that principle contained in Levit. xxv, 47, 48. We find in the civil Code, lib. i, tit. 10, "Judæus servum Christianum nec comparare debebit, nec largitatis aut alio quocumque titulo consequetur."

A Jew shall not purchase a Christian slave, nor shall he obtain one by title of gift, nor by any other title.

In a subsequent part of the title the penalty is recited, "non solum mancipii damno mulctetur, verùm etiam capitali sententia punietur." *Not only shall he be mulcted by the loss of the slave, but he shall be punished by a capital sentence.*

By a decree of Valentinian III, found after the Theodosian code, and entitled "De diversis ecclesiasticis capitibus," bearing date 425, Aquileia, vii of the ides of July, Jews and pagans were prohibited from holding Christian slaves.

Thus by the laws of the empire at this period no Jew or gentile could have any property in a Christian slave. We shall however see that this principle was not adopted until a much later period by the Franks and other nations, and this will account for the diversity of legislation and of judgment which the books of the same period exhibit in various regions.

Another clause of the code was more comprehensive, " Græcus, seu paganus, et Judæus, et Samaritanus, et alius hæreticus, id est, non existens orthodoxus, non potest Christianum mancipium habere." *A Greek or pagan, a Jew, a Samaritan, and any heretic, that is, one not orthodox, cannot hold a Christian slave.*

Another provision of the civil code regulated prohibitions of those customs which frequently were used by the Jews to ridicule the Christian ceremonies, lib. i, tit. ix, *De Judæis et Cœlicolis.* This law prohibited to Jews or pagans all rites in imitation of Christian ceremonies, or the use of the cross in any ceremonial of their own.

It was not unusual, at a much later period, for the Jews in some parts of Gaul where they were numerous, and indeed in parts of other regions, to insult the Christians in the holy week during the performance of some of their ceremonies, especially their processions; whence arose very serious riots and tumults, with all their bad consequences: to prevent which, as soon as the Catholics had power, they enacted laws of restraint, one of which is Canon xxx, of the third Council of Orleans, 538.

"Quia Deo propitio sub catholicorum regum dominatione consistimus, Judæi à die cænæ Domini usque in secundam Sabbati in Pascha, hoc est ipso quatriduo, procedere inter Christianos, neque Catholicis populis se ullo loco, vel quacumque occasione miscere præsumant."

Because through the mercy of God we are placed under the government of Catholic kings, let the Jews not presume to go among the Christians from Maunday Thursday to Easter Monday, that is, during four days; nor on any account any where to mingle with the Christian people.

The first Council of Macon on the Saone, in 581, in its Canon xiv, quotes the law of king Childebert for this prohibition, and states the reason, whilst it gives the prohibition a greater extent: "per plateas aut forum, quasi insultationis causâ deambulandi licentià denegetur"—*Let them not have liberty of walking through the streets or the market for the purpose of insult.*

Childebert died in 558.

I have thought it necessary to advert to these facts, and thus to state the law, to show the ground and the object of several enactments and judgments that will appear in my subsequent inquiry, and to show the various causes that led to modify slavery itself. I could have easily gone into more references, but this, I hope, will suffice.

We have, in a letter of Pope St. Gregory the Great to Libertinus the prefect of Sicily, evidence of the manner in which one of the Jews violated both the enactments of the civil code, viz., that which forbade the interference with the religious rites of Christians and that which rendered the Jew incapable of holding Christian slaves. The case into which he orders an inquiry was that of a man who, though of the Jewish nation, appears rather to have attempted the establishment of a new sect, or the mockery of Christianity, than the proselyting to the Jewish observances, for the Jewish ceremonial did not recognize such worship as he sought to introduce.

It must also be observed that at this period the authority of Gregory over Sicily was not, as at present, merely spiritual. He had a temporal supervision, if not a full sovereignty, over the island.

The document is Ep. xxxvii, lib. ii, indict. xi.

GREGORIUS Libertino Præfecto Siciliæ.

De præsumptione Nasæ Judæi, qui altare nomine B. Heliæ construxerat, et de mancipiis Christianis comparatis.

"Ab ipso administrationis exordio, Deus vos in causæ suæ voluit vindicta procedere, et hanc vobis mercedem propitius cum laude servavit. Fertur siquidem quòd Nasas quidam sceleratissimus Judæorum, sub nomine beati Heliæ altare puniendâ temeritate construxerit, multosque illic Christianorum ad adorandum sacrilegâ seductione decepit. Sed et Christiana, ut dicitur, mancipia comparavit, et suis ea obsequiis ac utilitatibus deputavit. Dum igitur severissimè in eum pro tantis facinoribus debuisset ulcisci, gloriosus Justinus medicamento avaritiæ, ut nobis scriptum est, Dei distulit injuriam vendicare. Gloria autem vestra hæc omnia districtâ examinatione perquirat: et si hujusmodi manifestum esse respererit, ita districtissime ac corporaliter in eundem sceleratum festinet vindicare Judæum; quatenus hâc ex causâ et gratiam sibi Dei nomine conciliet, et his se posteris pro suâ mercede imitandum monstret exemplis. Mancipia autem Christiana, quæcumque eum comparasse patuerit, ad libertatem, juxta legum præcepta, sine omni ambiguitate perducite, ne, quod absit, Christiana religio Judais subdita polluatur. Ita ergo omnia districtissimè sub omni festinatione corrigite, ut non solum pro hâc vobis disciplinâ gratias referamus, sed et testimonium de bonitate vestra ubi necesse fuerit, præbeamus."

GREGORY to Libertinus, Prefect of Sicily:

Concerning the presumption of Nasas, a Jew, who had erected an altar in the name of the blessed Elias ; and concerning the procuring of Christian slaves.

God has willed that from the very beginning of your administration you should proceed to the avenging of his cause; and he has mercifully kept this reward for you with praise. It is indeed said that one Nasas, a very wicked man, of the Jewish people, has, with a rashness deserving punishment, constructed an altar under the name of the blessed Elias, and deceitfully and sacrilegiously seduced many Christians thither for adoration. It is also said that he has procured Christian slaves, and put them to his service and profit. It has also been written to us that the most glorious Justin, when he ought to have most severely punished him for such crimes, has, through the soothing of his avarice, put off the avenging of this injury to God.

Do you, glorious sir, most closely examine into all the premises; and if you shall find the allegations evidently sustained, hasten to proceed most strictly to have bodily justice done upon this wicked Jew, so as to procure for yourself the favor of God in this case, and to exhibit for your reward, to those who will come after us, an example for imitation. But, farther, do you carry through, according to the prescriptions of the laws, to their liberty, without any cavilling, every and any Christian slaves that it may be evident he procured, lest, which God forbid, the Christian religion should be degraded by subjection to the Jews.

Therefore do all this correction most exactly and quickly, that you may not only have our thanks for preserving discipline, but that we may, when opportunity offers, give you proof of our recognition for your goodness.

I have before, in letter VII, quoted the thirty-first Canon of the fourth Council of Orleans, to show that the penalty of forfeiture of the slave was enacted by the Council, necessarily with the consent and by the authority of king Childebert, for only the civil power could make such a law when a Jewish owner attempted to make a proselyte of that slave. This shows that at that period the laws of the Franks allowed the Jews to possess Christian slaves.

The Canon xxx of the same council, to which I also alluded in the same letter, is the following:

"Cum prioribus canonibus jam fuerit definitum, ut de mancipiis Christianis, quæ apud Judæos sunt; si ad ecclesiam confugerint, et redimi se postulaverint, etiam ad quoscumque Christianos refugerint, et servire Judæis noluerint, taxato et oblato a fidelibus justo pretio, ab eorum dominio liberentur, ideo statuimus, ut tam justa constitutio ab omnibus Catholicis conservetur."

Whereas it has been decreed by former canons, respecting the Christian slaves that are under the Jews, that if they should fly to the church, or even to any Christians, and demand their redemption, and be unwilling to serve the Jews, they should be freed from their owners upon a fair price being assessed by the faithful and tendered for them: we therefore enact that this so just a regulation shall be observed by all Catholics.

Thus it is evident that at this period, 541, in this province and kingdom the Jew had a good title to his Christian slave, and could not be deprived of him except by law, or for value tendered, and this was acknowledged by the Council.

The reference to former Canons is principally to the thirteenth of the third Council of Orleans, to which I alluded in my letter VI.

The first Council of Macon was assembled at the request of King Guntram or Goutran, one of the sons of Clotaire I, to whom the division of Orleans was left upon the death of his father in 561. This assembly was held in 581. The portions of its canons which regarded temporalities had their sanction from the civil authority of the monarch.

The sixteenth canon is the following:

"Et licet quid de Christianis, qui aut captivitatis incursu, aut quibuscumque fraudibus, Judæorum servitio implicantur, debeat observari, non solum canonicis statutis, sed et legum beneficio pridem fuerit constitutum: tamen quia nunc ita quorumdam querela exorta est, quosdam Judæos, per civitates aut municipia consistentes in tantam insolentiam et proterviam prorupisse, ut nec reclamantes Christianos liceat vel precio de eorum servitute absolvi. Idcirco præsenti concilio, Deo auctore, sancimus, ut nullus Christianus Judæo deinceps debeat servire; sed datis proquolibet bono mancipio xii, solidis, ipsum mancipium quicumque Christianus seu ad ingenuitatem, seu ad servitium, licentiam habeat redimendi: quia nefas est, ut quod Christus dominus sanguinis effusione redemit persecutorum vinculis maneant irretiti. Quod si acquiescere his quæ statuimus quicumque Judæus noluerit, quamdiu ad pecuniam constitutam venire distulerit, liceat mancipio ipsi cum Christianis, ubicumque voluerit habitare. Illud etiam specialiter sancientes, quod si qui Judæus Christianum mancipium ad errorem Judaicum convictus fuerit persuassisse, ut ipso mancipio careat, et legandi damnatione plectetur."

And although the mode of acting in regard to Christians who have been entangled in the service of the Jews by the invasions for making captives, or by other frauds, has been regulated heretofore not only by canonical enactments, but also by favor of the civil laws; yet because now the complaint of some persons has arisen, that some Jews dwelling in the cities and towns have grown so insolent and bold that they will not permit the Christians demanding it to be freed even upon the ransom of their service, wherefore, by the authority of God, we enact by this present act of council that no Christian shall henceforth lawfully continue enslaved to a Jew; but that any Christian shall have the power of redeeming that slave either to freedom or to servitude, upon giving for each good slave the sum of twelve shillings (solidum): because it is improper that they whom Christ redeemed by the shedding of his blood, should continue bound in the chains of persecutors. But if any Jew shall be unwilling to acquiesce in these enacted provisions, it shall be lawful for the slave himself to dwell where he will, with Christians, as long as the Jew shall keep from taking the stipulated money. This also is specially enacted, that if any Jew shall be convicted of having persuaded his Christian slave to the adoption of Jewish error, he shall be deprived of the slave and amerced to make a gift.

Thus it was only at this period that we find any of the laws of the Franks introducing the right of a Christian to refuse service to a Jew. This however was not the case in all the territory, for that over which Guntram ruled was but a fourth part of the empire of this people.

We now proceed to examine another document of Pope Gregory the Great respecting Etruria. The town of Luna was in the Ligurian region, at the mouth of the river Macra, now la Magra. In or about 856 it became too inconsiderable to be continued a bishop's see, and its diocess was united to the territory belonging to the see of Sarzana, about five miles higher up on the river.

The following is Ep. xxi, lib. iii, indic. xii.

GREGORIUS, *Venantio Episcopo Lunensi:*

Quod Judæi non possunt Christiana habere mancipia: sed coloni et originarii pensiones illis præbere debent.

"Multorum ad nos relatione pervenit, a Judæis in Lunensi civitate degentibus, in servitio Christiana detineri mancipia: quæ res nobis tanto visà est asperior, quanto ea fraternitati tuæ patientia operabatur. Oportebat quippe te respectu loci tui, atque Christianæ religionis intuitu, nullam relinquere occasionem, ut superstitioni Judaicæ, simplices animæ non tam suasionibus, quam potestatis jure quodammodo deservirent. Quamobrem hortamur fraternitatem tuam, ut secundum piissimarum legum tramitem, nulli Judæo liceat Christianum mancipium in suo retinere dominio. Sed si qui penes eos inveniuntur, libertas eis tuitionis auxilio ex legum sanctione servetur. Hi vero qui in possessionibus eorum sunt, licet et ipsi ex legum districtione sint liberi; tamen quia colendis eorum terris diutius adhæserunt, utpote conditionem loci debentes, ad colenda quæ

consueverant rura permaneant, pensionesque prædictis viris præbeant: et
cuncta quæ de colonis vel originariis jura præcipiunt, peragant, extra quod
nihil eis oneris amplius indicatur. Quodsi quisquam de his vel ad alium
migrare locum, vel in obsequio suo retinere voluerit, ipse sibi reputet, qui
jus colonarium temeritate suâ, jus vero juris dominii sui severitate damna-
vit. In his ergo omnibus ita te volumus solerter impendi, ut nec direpti
gregis Pastor reus existas, nec apud nos minor æmulatio fraternitatem
tuam reprehensibilem reddat."

GREGORY *to Venantius, bishop of Luna :*

That Jews should not have Christian slaves, but that colonists and those
born on their lands should pay them pensions.

*We have learned by the report of many persons that Christian slaves are
kept in servitude the Jews dwelling in the city of Luna, which is the more
grievous to us as it has been caused by the remissness of you our brother.
For it was becoming you , as well by reason of the place you hold, as from
your regard or the Christian religion, not to allow the existence of any
occasion by which simple souls may be subjected to the Jewish superstition,
not only by the force of persuasion, but by a sort of right arising from
power. Wherefore we exhort you, our brother, that, according to the regulation of the most pious laws, it should not be permitted to any Jew to keep
a Christian slave under his dominion, and that if any such be found under
them, the liberty of such should be secured by the process of law and the aid
of protection.*

*And as regards those who are on their lands, though by strict construc-
tion of law they may be free, yet, because they have remained a long time in
the cultivation of the soil, as bound to the condition of the place, let them
remain to till the lands as they have used to do, and pay their pension to
the aforesaid men; and let them do all that the laws require of colonists or
persons of origin. Let no additional burthen however be laid on them.*

*But should any one of these desire to migrate to another place; or should
he prefer remaining in his obedience, let the consequences be attributed to him
who rashly violated the colonial rights, or who injured himself by the severity of his conduct towards his subject.*

*It is our wish that you be careful so to give your attention to all these
matters as not to be the guilty pastor of a plundered flock, nor that your
want of zeal should compel us to reprehend our brother.*

It may not be amiss now, viewing this document, to bring more closely
under our eye the law of the empire which was in force through Italy and
Sicily.

1. Slaves who were Christians could not be held by those who were not
Christians.

2. It being unlawful for others than Christians to hold them, these others could have no property in them : the persons so held were entitled to their freedom.

3. The church was the guardian of their right to freedom, and the church acted through the bishop.

4. Consequently it was the duty, as it was the right, of the bishop to vindicate that freedom for those so unjustly detained.

5. The right and duty of the pope was to see that each bishop was careful in his charge, and this part of his charge came as much as any other did under the supervision of his natural superior and immediate inspector, and it was the duty of that superior to reprehend him for any neglect.

6. The law of each country was to regulate the duty of the master and slave, and if that law made, as in Italy and its environs it did, the church the proper tribunal for looking to the performance of those duties, any neglect of the church in its discharge would be criminal.

7. Through the greater part of Italy and Sicily, at this period, the pope was in fact virtually, if not openly and fully, the sovereign, and it was only by his paramount influence that the half civilized Gothic and Lombard chiefs were kept in any order, and their despotism partially restrained.

They were times of anarchy, between which and the present no analogy exists. The Jews and separatists from the church were very numerous, and on their side, as well as on that of their opposers, passion frequently assumed the garb of religion, and the unfortunate slave was played upon by each. The position of the pope was exceedingly difficult, for whilst he had to restrain the enemies of the church on one side, he had to correct the excesses of its partizans upon the other. In my next letter I shall exhibit, for the purpose of placing the conduct of the pope in its proper point of view, some documents calculated to sustain the assertions I have here made.

I shall for the present conclude by giving the substantial distinctions found in the civil law between some classes of those called "conditionati" or "*persons under condition.*"

The "coloni," or "*colonists,*" were persons who were bound to the soil and could not leave it ; if the land was sold, they were sold with it, and their descendants were also fastened to the soil. They had the use of the ground upon certain conditions ; generally the payment of a certain rent in money, or the giving of a certain proportion of the produce, or a stipulated quantity without regard to proportion. They were distinguished into "originarii," *persons of origin,* that is, born on the ground, or "adscriptitii," *adopted* or written to it. The "advena," or *stranger* coming upon the ground and fulfilling the conditions without any special bargain, was prescribed against after thirty years, so that he thereby was legally a colonist without any farther formality. Or if he chose at once to become a colonist, it was done by a written instrument in duplicate between him and the lord of the soil, that is, by a pair of indentures.

In the case of the colonists of Luna it would appear that, if they were not legally prescribed against, there was what the pope considered to be equitable claim on the part of the Jewish owners of the soil to their services; but that if any one of them chose to use his right of going elsewhere, it must be seen that the original wrong was on the side of the landholder, who sought to bind to his service a person whom the law prevented from being his servant, or the pope supposed that it would not probably happen that the colonist would use his right of departing if he were not badly used. And therefore, relying on the continuance of kind feelings, he advised the bishop to allow the colonists to continue without the destruction of their legal right of self-deliverance; whilst he required of the prelate the performance of his duty in procuring the release of the slave illegally detained in bondage.

I dwell longer on this epoch, not only because I herein find more ample matter, but because at this period we discover serious alterations which greatly influenced the subsequent policy of Europe.

I have the honor to be, sir,

Respectfully, &c.

† JOHN, *Bishop of Charleston.*

CHARLESTON, S. C., *Jan.* 14, 1841.

LETTER XI.

To THE HON. JOHN FORSYTH, SECRETARY OF STATE, U. S.

SIR,—I stated in my last, that I felt it necessary in order to set the character of Pope St. Gregory the Great in a proper light, to give some documents which would show that he was as ready to restrain the excesses of the partizans of the church, and to protect the Jews, where they deserved protection, as he was to vindicate for the Christian slave his legal right to freedom, against the Jew that attempted to hold him irregularly in bondage.

I shall first exhibit his letter to an agent of the Holy See in Sicily. It is found Lib. vii, Indic. ii, Ep. lix.

GREGORIUS Fantino defensori Panormitano :
De synagogis Judæorum irrationabiliter occupatis.

" Ante aliquantum tempus Victori fratri et coepiscopq nostro scripsimus, ut quoniam quidam Judæorum datâ nobis petitione questi fuerunt, Synagogas in civitate Panormitanâ positas cum hospitiis suis fuisse ab eo irrationabiliter occupatas, qùousque causa utrum justè factum esset, potuisset agnosci, ab eorum se suspenderet congregatione : ne forte in eorum solâ voluntate versari præjudicium videretur. Et quidem nos prædictum fratrem nostrum incongrùe aliquid egisse, sacerdotii ejus respectus facile credere non permisit. Sed quia Salerio notario nostro, qui illic præsens postea inventus est, renunciante comperimus, nullam extitisse causam pro quâ potuissent rationabiliter occupari, atque eas esse inconsultè ac temerè consecratas : idcirco experientiæ tuæ præcipimus, ut quod semel consecratum est, Judæis ultra non valet restitui, quàntuum filiis gloriosio Venantio Patricio et Urbicio Abbate, synagogæ ipsæ cum his hospitiis quæ sub ipsis sunt, vel earum parietibus cohærent, atque hortis ibi conjunctis æstimatæ fuerint, studii tui sit, ut præfatus frater et coepiscopus noster dare pretium debeat ; quatenus hoc quod occupari fecit, in jus ecclesiæ ipsius valeat provenire, et illi opprimi, aut aliquam pati injustitiam nullo modo videantur. Codices vero vel ornamenta pariter ablata quærantur. Quæ si manifestè tulta sunt, et ipsa sine ambiguitate aliquâ volumus restitui : quia sicut illis quidquam in synagogis suis facere, ut et ipsi priùs scripsimus, ultra quàm lege decretum est, non debet esse licentia ; ita eis contra justitiam et æquitatem nec præjudicium, nec aliquod debet inferri dispendium."

GREGORY to Fantinus the Proctor at Palermo :
Concerning the Synagogues of the Jews unreasonably taken possession of.

" We have sometime back written to Victor our brother and fellow bishop ; because some Jews in their petition to us complained that he had unreasonably taken possession of their synagogues with their dwellings thereto attached in the city of Palermo, that he should suspend using them for divine offices (*congregatione*) until the case should be examined so as to ascertain whether this was justly done, lest it may seem that the injury was done to them by mere wilfulness. And indeed the respect irt which we hold his priesthood did not permit us easily to believe that our aforesaid brother had done any thing unbecoming.

" But since we have found by the report of Salerius our Notary who has been there subsequently, that there existed no reasonable cause for their being taken away : and that they were indiscreetly and rashly consecrated : we therefore command you, a man of experience, because that which has been once consecrated cannot any more be restored to the Jews ; that it be your duty to see what amount shall be assessed by our sons Venantius

Patrick and the Abbot Urbicius, as the value of the Synagogues themselves together with the dwellings that are under them or united to their walls, and the gardens belonging thereto ; so that our aforesaid brother and fellow bishop should give for them that price ; so that what he caused to be taken should become the property of the church, and that they (the Jews) should by no means appear to suffer any injustice or be oppressed. Let the books and ornaments that were taken away be sought after : which, if they have been evidently taken away, we desire to be restored without any quibbling : and as we have before written that no license should be given them to do in the Synagogues any thing beyond what is regulated by law, so that on the other hand, there should not be done to them any damage or prejudice in violation of either justice or of equity."

The above document shows that if the bishop in Etruria was censured for not doing his duty to the Christians illegally in bondage by Jews, the same Pope was equally ready to censure another bishop, who in Sicily, treated the Jews unjustly, and to order not only compensation for their loss, but restitution of such portion of their goods as could be returned, and protection against illegal or unjust acts.

The letter to which Pope St. Gregory refers, is found in Lib. vii, Ind. 1. Epist. xxvi, and is the following :—

GREGORIUS, Victori Episcopo Panormitano :

De Judæis non opprimendis injustè.—" Sicut Judæis non debet esse licentia quidquam in synagogis suis ultrà quàm permissum est a lege præsumere : ita in his quæ iis concessa sunt, nullum debet præjudicium sustineri. Quæ autem nobis in hâc urbe Romanâ habitantes Hebræi pro his qui Panormi degunt, conquesti sunt, data vos ab eis petitio quæ in subditis tenetur informat. Si igitur queremonia eorum veritate fulcitur ; oportet ut fraternitas vestra, legis serie diligenter inspectâ, ita eis quidquid hâc de

decretum est, custodire debeat ac servare, ut nec ipsa aliquid injustum facere nec illi pati præjudicium vi de antur. Si verò est aliquid quod ad restituendum ea quæ sunt postulata rationabiliter possit obsistere, judices à partibus eligantur, qui ea quæ æquitati conveniunt valeant definire. Quod si fortè illic contentio ipsa finiri nequiverit ; quatenus sine vestrâ invidiâ, quæ amica justitiæ visa fuerint decernantur. Quousque ergo causa ipsa finem accipiat, à consecratione locorum quæ ablata dicuntur, fraternitas se vestra suspendat."

GREGORY to Victor, Bishop of Palermo.

Of not unjustly oppressing the Jews.—" As it is not proper that license should be given to the Jews to presume to do anything in their Synagogues beyond what is permitted by law : so in those things which are conceded

" The accompanying petition which has been presented to us by Hebrews dwelling in this city of Rome on behalf of those who live at Palermo, will show you of what they complain. If then their complaints be founded on truth; it is fit that you, our brother, having diligently looked into the provisions of the law, should keep and observe, in their regard, all that is therein decreed ; so that you should appear to do nothing unjust, and they not to suffer any prejudice. If then there be any reasonable ground of objection to restoring those things which are demanded ; let judges be chosen by each of the parties to determine what shall be according to equity. But, if perchance, the litigation cannot be thus terminated; (the cause must come up to ourself) :* so that what shall appear befitting justice may be decreed without any suspicion being cast upon you. Meantime, until the cause shall be decided, do you, our brother, suspend any process to consecrate what is alleged to have been taken away."

The next letter in the same book is one to the same proctor, and shows the manner in which the Pope's tribunal was equally open to the Jew as to the Christian.

Epist. lx.

Gregorius, Fantino defensori :

De Jamno Judæo.—" Indicavit nobis Jamnus Judæus præsentium portitor, navem suam atque res suas Candidum defensorem nostrum cum aliis creditoribus occupasse, atque eas pro creditâ quam dederant pecuniâ venumdedisse, et a cunctis debitis cautionibus restitutis solùm apud se præfatum defensorem obligationis chirographum tenuisse, et sæpiùs se supplicantem ideo reddere contempsisse, quia, ut ait, sors debiti est satisfacta. Experientiæ ergo tuæ præcipimus, ut cum omni subtilitate curet addiscere : et si ita repererit, districtâ, compulsione perurge ; quàtenus omni morâ postpositâ, cautionem prædicti portitoris restituat. Ita ergo sollicitudo tua studeat, ut denùo ad nos hac de causâ querela non redeat."

Gregory to the Proctor Fantinus :

Concerning Jamnus the Jew.—" The Jew Jamnus the bearer of these presents, has exhibited to us that our proctor Candidus with other creditors have seized upon his ship and chattels, and have sold them for money that they lent to him, and that the aforesaid proctor kept back from amongst all the other securities that he restored to him, his written bond, and that he treated with contempt the several supplications which this man made for its return, upon the allegation that the principal of the debt was satisfied. We therefore command you, experienced sir, that you take heed to learn the facts with all exact sharpness, and if you shall find them as stated, press with very strict compulsion, so that without any delay whatever the proctor shall restore the security of the aforesaid bearer. So let your careful industry take heed that no complaint comes back again to us upon this case.

I shall now exhibit a document, showing not only the pope's own disposition to avoid using forcible means to procure a seeming conversion to the church, but also proving very manifestly the care which the Jews had to prevent any improper efforts at proselytism to Christianity, and their success in the applications which they for this purpose made to the holy see.

It is a letter to the archbishop of Arles, in the south-east part of France, and to the bishop of Marseilles, who was one of his suffragans. Both were men remarkable for piety and zeal. The letter is found lib. i, indi. ix, Ep. xlv.

GREGORIUS, Virgilio Arelatensi et Theodoro Episcopo Massiliæ Galliarum.

Ne Judæi vi baptizarentur, sed ad fidem amplectendam moneantur.

"Scribendi ad fraternitatem vestram reddendique debitæ salutationis alloquium, licet nullâ congrui temporis vel personarum esset occasio : actum est ut uno in tempore et quæ decebant de dilectione proximitatis fraternæ persolverem, et quorundam querimoniam, quæ ad nos perlata est, quomodo errantium animæ salvandæ sint, non tacerem. Plurimi siquidem Judaicæ religionis viri in hac provinciâ commorantes, ac subinde in Massiliæ partes pro diversis negotiis ambulantes, ad nostram perduxère notitiam multos consistentium in illis partibus Judæorum, vi magis ad fontem baptismatis quam prædicatione perductos. Nam intentionem quidem hujuscemodi et laude dignam censeo, et de Domini nostri dilectione descendere profiteor. Sed hanc eandem intentionem, nisi competens Scripturæ sacræ comitetur effectus timeo ne aut mercedis opus exinde non proveniat, aut juxta aliquid, animarum, quas eripi volumus, quod absit, dispendia subsequantur. Dum enim quispiam ad baptismatis fontem non prædicationis suavitate, sed necessitate pervenerit, ad pristinam superstitionem remeans, inde deteriùs moritur, unde renatus esse videbatur. Fraternitas ergo vestra hujusmodi homines frequenti prædicatione provocet : quatenus mutare veterem vitam de doctoris suavitate desiderent. Sic enim et intentio nostra recte perficitur, et conversi animus ad priorem denùo vomitum non mutatur. Adhibendus est ergo illis sermo, et qui errorum in ipsis spinas urere debeat, et prædicando quod in his tenebrescit illuminet ; ut pro his admonitione frequenti mercedem fraternitas vestra capiat, et eos quantum Deus donaverit, ad novæ regenerationem vitæ perducat."

GREGORY to Virgil of Arles, and Theodore bishop of Marseilles in Gaul: That Jews should not be baptized by compulsion, but should be warned to embrace the faith.

Although there should be no occasion of fitting times or personal affairs for writing to our brethren, and of returning their address of becoming salutation, yet it so happens that we can at the same time repay what is due for the love of your fraternal relationship and not be silent regarding the complaint of certain persons which has been laid before us, as to the manner in which the souls of those who err may be saved.

Indeed, several men of the Jewish religion who dwell in this province, and who frequently journey to parts of Marseilles upon business, have brought to our cognizance that many of the Jews dwelling there are frequently led to the baptismal font, more by violence than by preaching.

I consider the intention of those concerned to be indeed praiseworthy, and I admit that it was derived from the love of our Lord ; but I fear that, unless a sufficient working of the spirit of the Holy Scripture should accompany this intention, that either a work of merit will not flow therefrom, or that in some measure, which God forbid, it would be followed by the loss of those souls that we would desire to save. For when any person comes to the fountain of baptism not by the sweetness of preaching, but by compulsion, returning to his former superstition, he dies in a worse way by means of that from which he seemed to receive regeneration. Do you, our brethren, then urge these men by frequent preaching, so that they may desire to change their old life rather by the persuasion of the teacher. So will our intention be well made perfect, and the disposition of the convert not be turned to his former vomit. There should be used to them, then, such a form of speech as would burn up the thorns of their errors, and by the preaching illuminate what is dark in them ; so that you our brethren may obtain a reward for your frequently admonishing them, and that God may according to his bounty bring them to the regeneration of a new life.

Besides the above, several similar are found amongst his epistles. Such as lib. i, ind. ix, Ep. xxxiv, to Peter, bishop of Terracina, wherein, upon the complaint of Joseph, a Jew, that the bishop prevented the Jews from celebrating their festivities in a particular place, but consented to their celebration in different location, and then expelled them from this second the pope reproves him for this unjust and unkind proceeding, and shows him how much more becoming and useful it would be to treat those who are estranged from Christian truth with mildness and affection. To the same purport is his Ep. xv, lib. xi, indic. vi, to Paschasius, bishop of Naples, desiring that he would not permit any molestation of the Jews of that city, who complained to the pope that they were prevented from the celebration of their festivals in the manner that they and their fathers had been accustomed to have them solemnly observed. Gregory tells them that too frequently this interference is the effect of human passion, and not the offspring of zeal. Nam quicumque aliter agunt, et eos sub hoc velamine à consuetâ ritûs sui volunt cultura suspendere suas, illi magis quàm Dei causas probantur attendere.

This spirit of affection and persuasion breathes also in his letter to the proctor Faustinus, lib. vii, ind. 1, Ep. xxiv, in which he gives directions how he is to act regarding a number of Jews in the vicinity of Agrigentum or Girgenti, in Sicily, concerning whose good dispositions Domnina, the abbess of St. Stephen's monastery in that region, had written to him.

The truth of his observation respecting human passion assuming the garb of zeal, is clearly sustained by the contents of one of his letters to Januarius, bishop of Cagliari, in Sardinia, lib. vii, ind. 2, Ep. v, wherein he admonishes him to apply a proper remedy to the misconduct of one Peter, who, being newly converted from Judaism to Christianity, gave great scandal on Easter Sunday, the very day succeeding that of his baptism. Leading a mob of ill-conducted persons, contrary to the advice and remonstrances of the good and the religious, this fanatic or rogue, whichever he was, rushed to the synagogue, erected in it a cross and an image of the blessed virgin, and hung up there his own baptismal garment, though the bishop had, from a suspicion of his character, forewarned him against insulting those whom he left.

The Jews of Cagliari sent a deputation to complain of this to the pope, and the deputies carried with them the certificate of the governor, of the military commander, and of other noble persons, showing the truth of the facts charged. The letter of the pope requires that the Jews shall receive their synagogue and legal protection, that this Peter shall be restrained, his associates censured, the Catholics admonished, the cross, the image, and the robe be removed, and their synagogue left to the Jews. The bishop is praised for his opposition to the misconduct, and kindness and charity are inculcated.

In book xii, indic. vii, Epist. xviii, we have a letter of this pope to two bishops, Bacauda and Agnellus, commissioning them to examine the site of a synagogue at Terracina, for the possession of which the Jews had petitioned that they might have the papal sanction. It was represented to him that it was so near the church that their chaunting was heard from one in the other. He desires that the aforesaid bishops, together with the bishop of Terracina, shall, if such be the case, find another convenient site within the town where the Jews could observe their solemnities; and forbids that they should on any account be molested or burthened, but that in all things they should have ample justice according to the Roman law, but that they be not permitted to have Christian slaves.

I shall now exhibit a document showing the manner in which, by preventing the extensive introduction of even pagan slaves by the Jews, the increase of slavery was restrained. It gave to every Jewish or pagan slave of a Jew, in those places where the law was in force, the strongest inducement to make a profession of the Christian religion, whether in sincerity or in hypocrisy. It is found in lib. v, indic. xiv, Epist. xxxi.

GREGORIUS, Fortunato Episcopo Neopolitano.

Ne mancipïa quæ Christianum fidem suscipere volunt, Judæis venundentur : sed pretium à Christiano emptore percipiant.

"Fraternitati vestræ ante hoc tempus scripsimus, ut hos qui de Judaicâ superstitione ad Christianam fidem Deo aspirante venire desiderant, Dominis eoram nulla esset licentia venumdandi : sed ex eo quo voluntatis suæ desiderium prodidissent, defendi in libertatem per omnia debuissent. Sed quia quantum cognovimus, nec voluntatem nostram, nec legum statuta subtili scientes discretione pensare, in paganis servis hâc se non arbitrantur conditione constringi : fraternitatem vestram oportet de his esse solicitam, et si de Judæorum servitio non solum Judæos, sed etiam quisquam paganorum fieri voluerit Christianus, postquam voluntas ejus fuerit patefacta, nec hunc sub quolibet ingenio vel argumento cuipiam Judæorum venundandi facultas sit : sed is qui ad Christianam converti fidem desideret, defensione vestrâ in libertatem modis omnibus vindicetur. Hi vero quos hujusmodi oportet servos ammittere, ne forsitan utilitates suas irrationabiliter æstiment impediri, sollicitâ vos hæc convenit consideratione servare : ut si paganos, quos mercimonii causâ, de externis finibus emerint, intra tres menses dum emptor cui vendi debeant, non invenitur, fugiere ad ecclesiam forte contigerit, et velle se fieri dixerint Christianos, vel etiam extra ecclesiam hanc talem voluntatem prodederint, pretium ibi à Christiano scilicet emptore percipiant. Si autem post præfinitos tres menses quisquam hujusmodi servorum velle suum edixerit, et fieri voluerit Christianus, nec aliquis eum postmodum emere, nec dominus quâlibet occasionis specie audeat venundare, sed ad libertatis procul dubio præmia perducatur : quia hunc non ad vendendum, sed ad serviendum sibi intelligitur comparasse. Hæc igitur omnia fraternitas vestra ita vigilanter observet, quatenus ei nec supplicatio quorumdam valeat, nec persona surripere."

GREGORY *to Fortunatus, Bishop of Naples :*

That slaves who wish to embrace the Christian faith must not be sold to Jews, but (the owners) may receive a price from a Christian purchaser.

" We have before now written to you, our brother, that their masters should not have leave to sell those who, by the inspiration of God, desire to come from the Jewish superstition to the Christian faith ; but that from the moment they shall have manifested this determination they should be, by all means, protected to seek their liberty. But, as we have been led to know some persons, not exactly and accurately giving heed to our will, nor to the enactments of the laws, think that, as regards pagan slaves, this law does not apply, it is fit that you, our brother, should be careful on this head ; and if amongst the slaves of the Jews not only a Jew, but any of the pagans should desire to become a Christian, to see that no Jew should have power to sell him under any pretext, or by any ingenious device, after this his intention shall have been made known ; but let him who desires to become of the Christian faith have the aid of your defence, by all means, for his liberty.

" And respecting those who are to lose such servants, lest they should consider themselves unreasonably hindered, it is fit that you should carefully follow this rule : that, if it should happen that pagans whom they brought from foreign places for the purpose of traffic, should within three months, not having been purchased, fly to the church and say that they desire to be Christians, or even make known this intention without the church, let the owners be capable of receiving their price from a Christian purchaser. But if, after the lapse of three months, any one of those servants of this description should speak his will and wish to become a Christian, no one shall thereafter dare to purchase him, nor shall his master under any pretext sell him ; but he shall unquestionably be brought to the reward of liberty, because it is sufficiently intelligible that this slave was procured for the purpose of service, and not for that of traffic. Do you, my brother, diligently and closely observe all these things, so that you be not led away by any supplication, nor affected by personal regard."

The grounds of the law above given may be partially gathered from the following, which is a letter to the bishop of Catania in Sicily. Lib. v, ind. xiv, Epist. xxxii.

GREGORIUS, Leoni Episcopo Catanensi :
De Samaræis qui pagana mancipia emerunt et circumciderunt.

" Res ad nos detestabilis, et omnino legibus inimica pervenit, quæ si vera est, fraternitatem vestram vehementer accusat, qui eam de minori solicitudine probat esse culpabilem.

" Competimus autem quod Samaræi degentes Catinæ, pagana mancipia emerint, atque ea circumcidere ausu temerario præsumpserint. Atque idcirco necesse est, ut omnimodo zelum in hâc causâ sacerdotalem exercens, cum omni hoc vivacitate ac solicitudine studeas perscrutari : et si ita repereris, mancipia ipsa sine morâ in libertatem modis omnibus vindica, et ecclesiasticam in eis tuitionem impende, nec quidquam Dominos eorum de pretio quolibet modo recipere patiaris : qui non solù hoc damno-

GREGORY to Leo, Bishop of Catania:

Concerning Samaritans (or Jews) who purchased pagan slaves and circumcised them.

"Accounts have been brought to us of a transaction very detestable and altogether opposed to the laws, and which, if true, shows exceedingly great neglect on the part of you, our brother, and proves you to have been very culpable.

"We have found that some Jews dwelling at Catania have bought pagan slaves, and with rash presumption dared to circumcise them. Wherefore it is necessary that you should exert all your priestly zeal in this case, and give your mind to examine closely into it with energy and care; and, should you find the allegation to be true, that you should by all means, and without delay, secure the liberty of the slaves themselves, and give them the protection of the church; nor should you suffer their masters, on any account, to receive any of the price given for them, for they not only should be fined in this amount, but they are liable also to suffer such other punishment as the laws inflict."

I shall in my next endeavor to conclude the documentary evidence which I think useful to extract from the mass that is contained in the writings of St. Gregory the Great, and meantime

I have the honor to be, sir,

Respectfully, &c.

† JOHN, <i>Bishop of Charleston.</i></div>

CHARLESTON, S. C., <i>January 20th</i>, 1841.

LETTER XII.

To THE HON. JOHN FORSYTH, SECRETARY OF STATE, U. S.

SIR,—In my third letter I showed under the fifth head that in Judea the creditor could take the children of the debtor, and keep them as his slaves to labor until the debt was paid; and amongst the gentiles this right was not only in existence, but in most cases the child could be subjected to perpetual slavery, and in many instances the debtor himself could thus be reduced to bondage: and in fact, sir, I believe we could easily discover herein the origin of imprisonment for debt.

A serious improvement had been made in this respect, as will be seen by the following document, found in lib. iii, indic. xii, Epist. xliii.

Gregorius, Fantino Defensori :

De Cosma Syro multis debitis obligato.

" Lator præsentium Cosmas Syrus in negotio, quod agebat, debitum se contraxisse perhibuit, quod et multis aliis et lacrymis ejus attestantibus, verum esse credidimus.   Et quia 150 solidos debebat, volui ut creditores illius cum eo aliquid paciscerentur : quoniam et lex habet, ut homo liber pro debito nullatenus teneatur, si res defuerint, quæ possunt eidem debito addici, creditores ergo suos, ut asserit, ad 80 solidos consentire possibile est.   Sed quia multum est ut a nil habente homine 80 solidos petant, 60 solidos per notarium tuum tibi transmisimus, ut cum eisdem creditoribus subtiliter loquaris, rationem reddas, quia filium ejus quem tenere dicuntur, secundum leges tenere non possunt.   Et si potest fieri, ad aliquod minus quam nos dedimus, condescendant.   Et quidquid de eisdem 60 solidis remanserit, ipsi trade : ut cum filio suo exinde vivere valeat.   Si autem nil remanet, ad eamdem summam debitum ejus incidere stude, ut possit sibi libere postmodum laborare.   Hoc tamen solerter age : ut acceptis solidis ei plenariam munitionem scripto faciant."

Gregory, to the Proctor Fantinus :

Of Cosmas, the Syrian, deeply in debt.

" The bearer hereof, Cosmas the Syrian, has informed us that he contracted many debts in the business in which he was engaged.   We believe it to be true : he has testified it with many tears and witnesses.   And, as he owes 150 shillings, I wish his creditors would make some composition with him.   And as the law regulates that no freeman shall be held for a debt, if there be no goods which can be attached for that debt, he says that his creditors may be induced to accept 80 shillings ; but it is extravagant on their part to ask 80 shillings from a man who has nothing. We have sent you 60 shillings by your notary, that you may have a discreet conference with his creditors, and explain matters to them, because they cannot legally hold his son whom they are said to keep.   And if they will come down to any thing less, by your efforts, than the sum that we send, should any thing remain of the 60 shillings, give it to him to help to support himself and his son ; should nothing be left, exert yourself to have his debt cancelled by that amount sent, so that henceforth he may be free to exert himself for his own benefit.   But be careful, in doing this, to get for him a full receipt and discharge in writing for this money that they get."

The law to which the pope refers, and by which the persons of the unfortunate debtor and his family were protected, is found in *Novell.* 134, c. 7, and was enacted by Justinian I in 541.

Ne quis creditor filium debitoris pro debito retinere præsumat.

" Quia verò et hujuscemodi iniquitatem in diversis locis nostræ reipublicæ cognovimus admitti, quia creditores filios debitorum præsumunt retinere aut in pignus, aut in servile ministerium, aut in conductionem : hoc modis omnibus prohibemus : et jubemus ut si quis hujusmodi aliquid deliquerit, non solum debito cadat, sed tantam aliam quantitatem adjiciat dandam ei qui retentus est ab eo, aut parentibus ejus, et post hoc etiam corporalibus pœnis ipsum subdi a loci judice; quia personam liberam pro debito præsumpserit retinere aut locare aut pignorare."

That no creditor should presume to retain for debt the son of the debtor.

" And because we have known that this sort of injustice has been allowed in several places of our commonwealth,—that creditors presume to keep the children of their debtors, either in pledge or in slavish employment, or to hire them out,—we by all means forbid all this : and we order that, if any person shall be guilty of any of these things, not only shall he lose the debt, but he shall in addition give an equal sum, to be paid to the person that was held by him, or to the parents of such person ; and, beyond this, he shall be subjected to corporal punishment by the local judge, because he presumed to restrain or to hire out, or keep in pledge, a free person."

The ninth chapter of the same enactment prohibits the imprisonment of females for debt, or under process, or in any way under male custody.

The following document will exhibit in some degree the origin of the principle of escheats to be found in slavery. The slave being freed upon certain conditions, if they were not fulfilled the master of course re-entered upon his rights. The manumitted slave was sometimes allowed not only freedom, but a certain gift, and often with the condition that, if he had not lawful issue, the gift and its increase by his industry, should revert to the master or his heir. So in aftertimes the lord of the soil, or the monarch, gave portions of land to his vassals upon condition of service, and, upon failure of service or of heirs, his land escheated, or went back to the lord of the soil. It is curious that in many of our republics this slavish principle has extensive application.

The following document is found in lib. v, indic. xiv, Epist. xii.

GREGORIUS, Montanæ et Thomæ :

Libertatem dat, et eos cives Romanos efficit.

" Cum Redemptor noster totius conditor creaturæ ad hoc propitiatus humanam voluerit carnem assumere, ut divinitatis suæ gratia, dirupto quo tenebamur captivi vinculo servitutis, pristinæ nos restitueret libertati : salubriter agitur, si homines quos ab initio natura liberos protulit, et jus gentium jugo substituit servitutis, in eâ naturâ in quâ nati fuerant, manumittentis beneficio, libertati reddantur. Atque ideo pietatis intuitu, et hujus rei consideratione permoti, vos, Montanam atque Thomam famulos sanctæ Romanæ Ecclesiæ, cui, Deo adjutore, deservimus, liberos ex hac die, civesque Romanos efficimus, omneque vestrum vobis relaxamus servitutis peculium. Et quia tu Montana animum te ad conversionem fateris appulisse Monachicam : idcirco duas uncias, quas tibi quondam Gaudiosus presbyter per supremæ suæ voluntatis arbitrium institutionis modo noscitur reliquisse, hac die tibi donamus, atque concedimus omnia scilicet monasterio Sancti Laurentii cui Constantina Abbatissa præest, in quo converti Deo miserante festinas, modis omnibus profutura. Si quid vero de rebus suprascripti Gaudiosi te aliquomodo celasse constituerit, id totum ecclesiæ nostræ juri sine dubio mancipetur. Tibi autem suprascripto Thomæ, quem pro libertatis tuæ cumulo etiam inter notarios volumus militare, quinque uncias, quas præfatus Gaudiosus presbyter per ultimam voluntatem hereditario tibi nomine dereliquit, simul et sponsalia, quæ matri tuæ conscripserat, similiter hac die per hujus manumissionis paginam donamus, atque concedimus, eâ sane lege, atque conditione subnexâ, ut si sine filiis legitimis, hoc est, de legitimo susceptis conjugio, te obire contigerit, omnia quæ tibi concessimus, ad jus Sanctæ Romanæ Ecclesiæ sine diminutione aliquâ revertantur. Si autem filios de conjugio, sicut diximus, cognitos lege susceperis, eosque superstites reliqueris, earumdem te rerum dominum sine quadam statuimus conditione persistere, et testamentum de his faciendi liberam tibi tribuimus potestatem. Hæc igitur, quæ per hujus manumissionis Chartulam statuimus, atque concessimus, nos successoresque nostros, sine aliquâ scitote refragatione servare. Nam justitiæ, ac rationis ordo suadet, ut qui sua a successoribus desiderat mandata servari, decessoris sui proculdubio voluntatem et statuta custodiat. Hanc autem manumissionis paginam Paterio notario scribendam dictavimus, et propriâ manu una cum tribus presbyteris prioribus, et tribus Diaconis pro plenissimâ firmitate subscripsimus, vobusque tradidimus. Actum in urbe Româ."

GREGORY to Montana and Thomas.

He emancipates them, and makes them Roman citizens.

" Since our Redeemer, the maker of every creature, mercifully vouchsafed to take human flesh, that breaking the chain by which we were held captive, he may, by the grace of his divinity, restore us to our first liberty, it is then salutary that they whom he at first made free by nature, and whom the law of nations subjected to the yoke of slavery, should in the nature in which they were born be restored to liberty by that kindness of their emancipator. And therefore, moved by this consideration, and in respect to piety, we make you, Montana and Thomas, slaves of the holy

Roman church, in whose service we are by God's help engaged, from this day forward free and Roman citizens. And we release to you all your allowance of slavery.

" And because you, Montana, have declared that it was your wish to enter into the monastic state, we give and grant to you this day two ounces, which it is well known were formerly left as a legacy to you for inheritance by the priest Gaudiosus, to be by all means available to the monastery of St. Lawrence, over which Constantina is superioress, and into which you desire anxiously by God's mercy to be admitted. But should it appear that you have concealed any of the effects of the said Gaudiosus, the entire thereof doubtless is by right for the service of our church.

" But to you, the said Thomas, whom, in addition to the bestowal of freedom, we desire to be enrolled in service amongst our notaries, we likewise this day give and grant, by this charter of manumission, five ounces which the same Gaudiosus the priest left to you by name in his last will, and the portion which he assigned for your mother, but upon this ground and condition well attached, that, should you die without issue by lawful marriage, all those goods which we have granted to you shall come back, without any diminution, under the dominion of the holy Roman church ; but should you leave behind you children lawfully recognized from your marriage, we give to you full power to hold the same effects as their owner, and without any condition, and to make free disposition of the same by will.

" Know you, therefore, that what we have thus, by this charter of manumission enacted and granted to you, bind, without any gainsay, ourselves and our successors for its observance. For the order of justice and of reason requires that he who desires his own commands to be observed by his successors, should also doubtless observe the will and the statutes of his predecessor.

" We have dictated this writing of manumission to be copied by our notary Paterius, and have for its most perfect stability subscribed it with our hand, and with those of three of the more dignified priests and three deacons, and delivered them to you.

" Done in the city of Rome," &c.

One of the subjects which at all times caused slavery to be surrounded with great difficulties was the result of marriage. The interest of the owner frequently interfered with the affection of the husband and wife, and also was irreconcileable to the relation of parent and child. The liability to separation of those married was a more galling affliction in the Christian law, where the Saviour made marriage indissoluble, and it often happened that an avaricious or capricious owner cared as little for the marriage bond as he did for the natural tie of affection. Hence, as Christianity became the religion of the state, or of the great body of the people, it was imperatively demanded, by the very nature of the case, that some restraint should be placed upon that absolute power which the owners had, and sometimes abused, of wantonly making these separations. On the other hand, the association of the sexes made marriage desirable : it was ordained by God to be the general state of the bulk of mankind, and even the self-interest or the avarice of the master calculated upon its results. Then again the slave dreaded separation, not only because of the violence committed on the most sacred affections, but also because, though the husband and wife should be separated by impassable barriers, yet the bond of their union subsisted, and could be severed by death alone.

This was a strong temptation to both master and slave to prefer concubinage to wedlock. This is one of the worst moral evils attending slavery, where no restraint of law effects its removal.

Another difficulty arose, especially in cases of the colonist, by reason of the claims of the several owners where colonists of distinct estates and different owners intermarried. In the case of perfect slaves the child generally followed the mother, both as regarded condition and property. This was not however universally the case. But the owners of colonized lands set up different claims. At length the dispute was settled in the Roman empire by a law of Justinian, in 539, Novell. clxii, cap. 3, and confirmed by a decision in a case brought up by the church wardens of Apamea in Phrygia, in 541, on the kalends of March, by dividing equally the progeny between the estates to which the parents belonged, giving the preference, in all cases of uneven number, to that estate to which the mother was attached. Nov. clvii, tit. xxxix.

The following law concerning marriages and the separation of married persons from each other, and of children from their parents, is of the same date.

Novell. clvii. *De Rusticis qui in alienis prædiis nuptias contrahunt.*— Tit. xl.

Imp. Justin. August. Lazaro Comiti Orientis.

Præfatio. Ex his, quæ diverso modo ad nos relata sunt, didicimus in Mesopotamiâ et Osdroenâ provinciis quidquam delinqui, nostris plane temporibus indignum. Consuetudinem etiam apud ipsos esse, ut qui ex diversis originem trahant prædis, nuptias inter se contrahant. Inde sane conari dominos, de facto jam contractas nuptias dissolvere, aut procreatos filios a parentibus abstrahere, exindeque totum illum locum misere affligi, dum et rusticani viri et mulieres ex una parte distrahantur, et proles his adimitur, qui in lucem produxerunt, et solâ nostrâ opus esse providentiâ.

Cap. I. Sancimus igitur, ut prædiorum domini de cætero rusticos suos, prout voluerint, conservent : neque quisquam eos qui jam conjuncti sunt, possit secundum consuetudinem prius obtinentem divellere, aut compellere ut terram ad ipsos pertinentem colant, abstrahereve a parentibus filios prætextu conditionis colonariæ. Sed et si quid hujusmodi forte jam factum est : corrigi hoc simul, et restitui efficies, sive filios abstrahi contigerit, sive etiam mulieres, nempe vel a parentibus, vel contubernii consortibus : eo, qui reliquo deinceps tempore hujusmodi aliquid facere præsumpserit, etiam de ipso prædio in periculum vocando. Quare libera sunto contubernia metu, qui dudum ipsis immittitur, et parentes habento ex hac jussione filios suos : nequeuntibus prædiorum dominis subtilibus contendere rationibus, et vel nuptias contrahentes, vel filios abstrahere. Qui enim tale quid facere præsumpserit : etiam de ipso prædio in periculum veniet, cui eos vindicare rusticos attentat."

Epilogus.—" Quæ igitur nobis placuerunt, et per sacram hanc pragmaticam declarantur formam, eam providentiam habeto magnificentia tua, tibique obtemperans cohors, et qui pro tempore eundem magistratum geret, ut ad effectum deducantur conserventurque, trium librarum auri pœna imminenti ei, qui ullo unquam tempore hæc transgredi attentaverit. Dat. Kal. Maii, Constantinop. D. N. Justin. PP. Aug. Bisil. V. C. Cons."

" *Of Country persons who contract Marriage on divers estates.*"

" The Emperor Justinian Augustus, to Lazarus the Count of the East."

Preamble.—" We have learned by relation in various ways, that a delinquency quite unworthy of our times, is allowed in the provinces of Mesopotamia and of Osdroene. They have a custom of having marriage contracted between those born on different estates : whence the masters endeavor to dissolve marriages actually contracted, or to take away from the parents the children who are their issue; upon which account that entire place is miserably afflicted, whilst country people, husbands and wives, are drawn away from each other, and the children whom they brought into light are taken away from them ; and that there needs for the regulation only our provision."

Chapter I.—" Wherefore, we enact, that otherwise the masters of the aforesaid keep their colonists as they will ; but, it shall not be allowed by virtue of any custom heretofore introduced and in existence, to put away from each other those who are married, or to force them to cultivate the land belonging to themselves, or to take away children from their parents, under the color of colonial condition. And you will be careful that if any thing of this sort has haply been already done, the same be corrected and restitution made, whether it be that children were taken away from their parents or women from their consorts of marriage. And for any who shall in future presume to act in this way, it shall be at the hazard of losing the estate itself."

" Wherefore, let marriages of servants be exempt from that fear which has hitherto hung over them : and from the issue of this order, let the parents have their children. It shall not be competent for the lords of the estates to strive by any subtle arguments either to take away those who contract marriage, or their children. For he who shall presume to do any such thing shall incur the risk of losing that estate for which he attempts to claim those colonists."

EPILOGUE.—" That therefore which has been good in our view, and is declared by this sacred pragmatic form, let your magnificence provide to have carried into execution, and the cohort which obeys you, as also he who for the time being shall hold the same magisterial office. To the end then that this edict may produce its effect and continue in force, let him who may at any time violate its enactments be liable to a penalty of three pounds of gold."

" Given at Constantinople, on the Kalends of May, our most pious Lord Justinian, being Augustus, and the most renowned Basil being Consul."

This was an important amelioration of the worst feature of slavery : but, still the master's right to the labor was left untouched, whilst the rights of nature and of religion were secured to the colonist, and the transition from absolute slavery to the colonial condition was imperceptibly diminishing the number of those in the former and increasing those in the latter condition. It became a principle, where an estate was large and the colonists numerous, to confine the choice of the servants within the bounds of the property; and thus marriage had its full sanctity and families remained without separation.

We have an instance of the exercise of this right, by Pope St. Gregory, in a document found in Lib. X, Indic. v, Epist. 28.

GREGORIUS, Romano Defensori.

De filiis Petri defensoris extra massam in quâ nati sunt, non jungendis.

" Petrus quem defensorem fecimus, quia de massâ juris Ecclesiæ nostræ, quæ Vitelas dicitur, oriundus sit, experientiæ tuæ bene est cognitum. Et ideo quia circa eum benigni debemus existere, ut tamen Ecclesiæ utilitas non lædatur : hac tibi præceptione mandamus, ut eum districte debeas admonere, ne filios suos quolibet ingenio vel excusatione foris alicubi in conjugio sociare præsumat, sed in eâ massâ, cui lege et conditione ligati sunt, socientur. In quâ re etiam et tuam omnino necesse est experientiam esse sollicitam, atque eos terrere, ut qualibet occasione de possessione cui oriundo subjecti sunt, exire non debeant. Nam si quis eorum exinde, quod non credimus, exire præsumpserit; certum illi est quia noster consensus nunquam illi aderit, ut foris de massâ in quâ nati sunt, aut habitare aut debeant sociari, sed et superscribi terram eorum. Atque tunc sciatis vos non leve periculum sustinere, si vobis negligentibus quisquam ipsorum quidquam de iis quæ prohibemus, facere qualibet sorte tentaverit."

GREGORY to the Proctor Romanus.

Of not marrying the children of Peter the Proctor, without the limits of the estate upon which they were born.

"You, experienced sir, are well aware that Peter, whom We made a Proctor, is a native of the estate of our church territory which is called Vitelas. And as our desire is to act towards him with such favor as is compatible with avoiding any injury to the church; We command you by this precept, that you should strictly warn him not to presume under any pretext or excuse, to have his children joined in wedlock any where but on that estate to which they may be bound by law or by condition. In which matter it is quite necessary that you, experienced sir, be very careful and instil into them a fear to prevent any of them from going on any account beyond the estate to which they are subject by origin. For if any one of them shall presume, as we believe he will not, to go thence; let him be assured that he shall never have our consent either to dwell or to associate himself without the estate on which he was born, but that the land of any such person shall be more heavily charged (*Superscribi.*) And know you, that if by your negligence, any of them shall attempt to do any of those things which we prohibit, you will incur no small danger."

Many of the restrictions on marriage that are found in subsequent ages, under the feudal system, had their origin in this principle, because indeed the vassal, in feudal times, was but a slave, under a more loose dominion, in a mitigated form.

The following document shows, that, at least in the west, the separation of married persons was very uncommon, (quam sit inauditum atque crudele,) (*unheard of and cruel.*) It is found in Lib. III, Indic. xii, Epist. 12.

GREGORIUS, Maximiano Episcopo Syracusano.

De uxore cujusdam ablatâ et alteri venumdatâ.

" Tanta nobis subinde mala, quæ aguntur in istâ provinciâ, nunciantur; ut peccatis facientibus, quod avertat omnipotens Deus, celeriter eam perituram credàmus. Præsentium namque portitor veniens lacrymabiliter quæstus est, ante plurimos annos ab homine nescio quo de possessione Messanensis Ecclesiæ de fontibus se susceptum, et violenter diversis suasionibus puellæ ipsius junctum, ex quâ juvenculos filios jam habere se asseruit, et quam nunc violenter huic disjunctam abstulisse dicitur, atque cuidam alii venumdedisse. Quod si verum est, quam sit inauditum atque crudele malum, tua bene dilectio perspicit. Ideoque admonemus, ut hoc tantum nefas sub ea vivacite, quam te in causis piis habere certissime scimus, requiras atque discutias. Et si ita ut supradictus portitor insinuavit, esse cognoveris, non solum quod male factum est, ad statum pristinum revocare curabis; sed et vindictam, quæ Deum possit placare, exhibere modis omnibus, festinabis. Episcopum vero, qui homines suos talia agentes corrigere negligit atque emendare, vehementer aggredere, proponens, quia si denuo talis ad nos de quoquam qui ad eum pertinet, quærela pervenerit, non in eum qui excesserit, sed in ipsum canonice vindicta precedet."

GREGORY to Maximinian, Bishop of Syracuse.

Concerning the wife of some one that was taken away and sold to another.

" We are told of so many bad things done in that province, that we are led to believe, which may God forbid, the place must soon be destroyed.

" Now, the bearer of these presents complained to us in a pitiable manner, that many years ago some man whom I know not, belonging to the church of Messina stood as his sponsor at baptism, and prevailed upon him by extreme urgency to marry his servant, by whom, he says, he has now young children, and whom now this man has violently taken away and sold to another. If this be true, you, our beloved, will see plainly how unheard of and how cruel is the evil. We therefore admonish you to look into and to sift so great a crime, with that earnestness which we assuredly know you have in matters of piety: and should you come to know that the fact is, as the aforesaid bearer has stated, you will be careful not only to bring back to its former state that which was badly done, but you will quickly, by all means, have that punishment inflicted which may appease God. Give a severe lecture to the bishop that neglected to correct or to amend his people who do such things; setting before him that if a like complaint comes to us again of any one who belongs to him, canonical process for punishment shall issue, not against the one that shall have done wrong, but against himself."

This will, in conjunction with the other documents, then mark the close of the sixth century as a period when, after the blindness of paganism, the corruption which regarded concubinage with indifference, the impiety which would deprive matrimony of its influence and dignity, and notwithstanding the cruelty which in bad times was used towards the unfortunate slave in this regard, religion at length gave her benign aid to procure that authoritative legislation and a more generous policy should soften the rigors of slavery and begin to mitigate its evils by giving to this dependant upon his fellow-men the right to the holiest of those bonds by which parents and children were bound by the ties of religion, of nature, and of affection. We may therefore regard this as the period when after ages of difficulty, the Christian religion had vindicated for the slave this common right of secure marriage to which nature has given a claim which religion has always recognized. It is true, that though this right is considered inalienable, it is like every other to be regulated by restraints, which without the destruction or the serious injury of the right itself, may be found necessary for the good of the community.

I have the honor to be, sir,

Respectfully, &c.

† JOHN, *Bishop of Charleston.*

CHARLESTON, S. C., *January 28,* 1841.

LETTER XIII.

To THE HON. JOHN FORSYTH, SECRETARY OF STATE, U. S.

SIR,—I shall now wind up the examination of this epoch, upon which I have dwelt so long, by adducing a few more of the many documents that exhibit the belief of the Church in her practice at the period in question, respecting the right to property in slaves.

I have already, in my ninth letter, given the deed which Pope St. Gregory made, conveying a slave to Felix, bishop of Porto. I shall now give one similar thereto, which is found in Lib. II, Indic. xi, Epist. 18.

GREGORIUS, Theodoro Consiliario,

Acosimum puerum dat per epistolam.

" Ecclesiasticis utilitatibus desudantes Ecclesiasticâ dignum est remuneratione gaudere, ut qui se voluntariis obsequiorum necessitatibus spontè subjiciunt, dignè nostris provisionibus consolentur. Quia igitur te Theodorum virum eloquentissimum consiliarum nostrum, mancipiorum cognovimus ministerio destitutum ideo puerum nomine Acosimum, natione Siculum, juri dominioque tuo dari tradique præcipimus. Quem quoniam traditum ex nostrâ voluntate jam possides, hujus te necesse fuit scripti pro futuri temporis testimonio ac robore largitatis, auctoritate fulciri : quatenus Domino protegente, securè eum semper et sine ullius retractionis suspicione, quippe ut dominus, valeas possidere. Neque enim quemquam fore credimus, qui tam pervam largitatem pro tuâ tibi devotione concessam desideret, vel tentet ullo modo revocare : cum uno eodemque tempore, et verecundum sit a decessoribus benè gesta resolvere et verecumdum sit docere ceteros in suâ quandoque resolutoriam proferre largitate sententiam

Gregory, to Theodore the Counsellor.

He, by letter, gives him the boy Acosimus.

"It is fit that they who labor for the benefit of the Church should enjoy a reward from the Church, that they who voluntarily and of their own accord have undertaken burthensome duties should be worthily assisted by our provision. Because therefore, We have known that you, Theodore, our counsellor, a most eloquent man, were not well provided with the service of slaves, We have ordered that a boy, by name Acosimus, of the Sicilian nation, should be given up and delivered to your right and dominion. And as you already have him in your possession by delivery, upon our will, it was necessary to fortify you with the authority of this writing as a testimony to the future and for protection of the gift: so that by God's protection, you may have power to possess him as his lord and master, always securely for ever and without any question being raised of his being in any way taken back. Nor indeed, do We believe that there is any one who would desire or would attempt in any way to revoke so small a bounty given to you for your devotion. Since it would be shameful to undo the good deeds of our predecessors, as it would to teach others that each could from time to time make the revocation of his own gift."

The next document is found in Lib. X, Indic. v, Epist. 40.

Gregorius, Bonito Defensori,

De mancipio Fortunati Abbatis.

"Filius noster Fortunatus Abbas monasterii sancti Severini, quod in hâc urbe Romanâ situm est latores præsentium monachos suos illic pro recolligendis mancipiis juris sui monasterii quæ illic latitare dicuntur dirigens, petiit ut experientiæ tuæ ei debeant adesse solatia. Eâ propter præsenti tibi auctoritate præcipimus, ut eis in omnibus salvâ ratione concurrere ac opitulari festines : quatenùs te illic corâm posito, atque in hâc causâ ferente solatia, salubriter hæc citiùs valeant quæ sibi injuncta sunt, ad effectum, Deo auctore, perducere."

Gregory, to the Proctor Bonitus,

Concerning the slave of the Abbot Fortunatus.

"Our son Fortunatus, the Abbot of the monastery of St. Severinus which is in the city of Rome, directing his monks the bearers of these presents to your neighborhood to gather slaves belonging to the rights of his monastery, who are said to be there in concealment, begged that he should have your aid for that object. Wherefore, We command you, by this present order, that you would be alert in giving them all reasonable concurrence and aid ; so that you being present there and comforting them in this business, they may, with God's aid, be able in a wholesome manner the sooner to perform the duty which has been laid upon them."

Thus, Sir, the Pope did not consider it unbecoming in the monastery of St. Severinus to hold slaves, nor irreligious for the Abbot to send monks to bring back runaways, nor criminal for the monks to go looking for them, nor offensive to God, on his own part, to give letters to his officer and overseers to aid by all reasonable means to discover, and to capture them.

The following document appears perhaps to enter into more minute details for the recovery of a slave than you would calculate upon finding in this compilation. It is found in Lib. VII, Ind. ii, Epist. 107.

GREGORIUS Sergio Defensori.

De Petro puero fugâ lapso.

" Filius noster vir magnificus Occilianus, tribunus Hydruntinæ civitatis, ad nos veniens, puerum unum, Petrum nomine, artis pistoriæ, ex jure germani nostri, ad eum noscitur perduxisse. Quem nunc fugâ lapsum ad partes illas reverti cognovimus. Experientia ergo tua antequam ad Hydruntinam civitatem valeat is ipse contingere sub quâ valueris celeritate, vel ad episcopum Hydruntinæ civitatis, vel ad prædictam tribunum se vel alium quem in loco tuo te habere cognoscis, scripta dirigas, ut uxorem vel filios praedicti mancipii sub omni habere debeant cautelâ atque de ipso sollicitudinem gerere, ut preveniens valeat detineri, et mox cum rebus suis omnibus, quæ ad eum pertinent, navi impositis per fidelem personam huc modis omnibus destinari. Experientia itaque tua cum omni hoc studeat efficaciâ solertiaque perficere, ne de neglectu vel morâ nostros, quod non optamus, animos offendas."

GREGORY, to the proctor Sergius,

Concerning Peter, a servant who fled away.

" Our son Occilianus a highly respectable man, a tribune of the city of Otranto brought with him to our cousin, as is known, when he was coming to us, a boy named Peter, a baker, who belonged to that cousin. We have now learned that he has run away and returned to your country. Let then it be your care, experienced Sir, before he shall be able to get back to Otranto, to direct as quickly as you can, a writing to the Bishop of Otranto, or to the foresaid tribune himself or to any one else whom you know, that you can depute, to have a good care of the wife or children of the said slave, and to be very careful respecting himself, that as soon as he shall arrive he may be detained, and sent with every thing that pertains to him, by all means hither, embarking them on board a ship under care of some faithful person.

" You, experienced Sir, will therefore exert yourself to do this with all attention and effect, so as not to displease us by a delay or neglect, which we should not desire."

I shall place after this, the following taken from Lib. VIII, Indic. iii, Ep. 4.

GREGORIUS, Fantino Defensori.

De mancipiis Romani spectabilis viri.

" Mancipia juris Romani spectabilis memoriæ viri, qui in domo suâ quæ Neapoli sita est, monasterium ordinari constituit, habitare in Siciliâ perhibentur. Et quia monasterium ipsum juxta voluntatem ejus, Deo auctore, noscitur ordinatum, experientia tua præsentium portitoribus, qui ad recolligenda mancipia ipsa illuc directi sunt, omni studio solatiari festinet, et recollectis eis, possessiones illis ubi laborare debeant, te solatiante conducat. Et quidquid eorum labore accesserit, reservato unde ipsi possint subsistere, reliquam ad prædictum monasterium, experientiæ tuæ curâ, annis singulis, auxiliante domino, transmittantur."

GREGORY to the proctor Fantinus,

Concerning the slaves of the honorable man Romanus.

" The slaves of the man of honorable memory, Romanus, who directed that his house in Naples should be formed into a monastery, are said to dwell in Sicily. And as it is known that, with God's help, the monastery has been established according to the regulations of his will ; you, experienced Sir, will without delay use your best efforts to aid the bearers of these presents who are sent thither to collect those slaves ; and when they shall be collected, let them hire lands under your countenance, where they may labor ; keeping them out of their produce of labor whatever may be necessary for their support ; let the remainder, under the care of you, experienced Sir, be sent, with God's help, every year to the foresaid monastery."

GREGORIUS, Vitali defensori Sardiniæ,

De Barbaracinis mancipiis comparandis.

" Bonifacium præsentium portitorem, notarium scilicet nostrum, ad nos experientia tua illuc transmississe cognoscat, ut in utilitatem parochiæ, Barbaricina debeat mancipia comparare. Et ideo experientia tua omnino et studiose sollicitaque concurrat, ut bono pretio, et talia debeat comparare, quæ in ministerio parochiæ utilia valeant inveniti, atque emptis eis huc Deo protegente is ipse celerius possit remeare. Ita ergo te in hac re exhibere festina, ut te quasi servientium amatorem, quorum usibus emuntur, ostendas, et nobis ipsi te de tuâ voleant sollicitudine commendare."

GREGORY to Vitalis, proctor of Sardinia.

Of buying Barbary slaves.

" Know, experienced Sir, that Boniface our Notary, the bearer of these presents, has been sent by us to your place to purchase some

Barbary slaves for the use of the hospital. And therefore, you will be careful to concur diligently and attentively with him that he may buy them at a good rate and such as would be found useful for the service of the hospital. And that having bought them, he may, under the protection of God, very speedily return hither. Do you then be prompt to show yourself in this business so as to exhibit your affection for those who serve the hospital and for whose use the purchase is made, and that they may have it in their power to commend you to us for your zeal in their regard."

The word *parochiæ*, which is translated "hospital," is more properly *ptochia* in some of the ancient MSS. which is a sort of latinized imitation of πτωχία—a house for feeding the poor. St. Gregory had a large establishment of this description in Rome attended by pious monks, for whose service these barbarians were purchased. Procopius informs us; lib. ii, de bello Vandanco cap. 13, who these Barbary slaves were. When the Vandals had conquered the Moors of Africa, they were annoyed by the incursions of some of the barbarians of the southern part of Numidia. In order to prevent this, they seized upon themselves, their wives and children, and transported them to the island of Sardinia : kept prisoners and slaves for some time here, they escaped to the vicinity of Cagliari, and forming a body of 3,000 men, they regained a sort of freedom. St. Gregory made various efforts to convert them. They who were kept in thraldom were frequently purchased, as in this instance, by the Italians and others.

I have now, Sir, shown that in the Roman Catholic church, up to the beginning of the seventh century, though slavery lost many of its harsher and more cruel and repulsive characteristics, the possession, the purchase, the transfer and the disciplinary rule of slaves, was by no means incompatible with the most perfect piety and sublime practice of religion. This, Sir, is domestic slavery, as distinguished from the "slave trade." We have seen that the violent and rapacious incursions of pirates who carried off into captivity the defenceless inhabitants of an unsuspecting country, were condemned by the Pastors of that church, and when we shall arrive at the period when Portugal opened the way and gave origin to the modern slave trade, we shall see a repetition of the distinction between domestic slavery, and the slave trade, marked in the permission and in the censures of the church.

One of the documents which to me was the most interesting in the twelve books of letters which we have from the pen of this holy Pontiff, is the 41st of the eleventh book, to the Notary Pantaleon, in which he reminds that officer of the solemn oath that he took at the tomb of St. Peter, the prince of the Apostles, to discharge faithfully the office to which he was appointed in superintending the Papal patrimony in Syracuse. He then proceeds to applaud the conduct of Pantaleon who, as Valerius, one of the Pope's Secretaries, informed him, broke a measure which he found too large, and which had been used by some of the overseers in measuring the grain which the colonists were required to furnish. He then proceeds to state how the same Valerius informed him that Pantaleon had made a calculation of the amount in which he supposed the overseers had defrauded those servants, and thanks him for it. He then charges him upon his oath, not to have the Holy See a partaker of this fraud ; but to give to the poor colonists of each estate, cows, hogs or sheep, to the amount of the fraud committed by the false measure, and to call to his counsel for this purpose, the bishop, the local Secretary, and the Governor if convenient. He wishes them to determine whether it would be more advisable to make restitution to the colonists in gold or in stock. He concludes by stating that he has enough and does not want to be thus enriched, and solemnly warns him so to act, as that on the great day of judgment neither of them shall be deprived of their reward by reason of any fraud upon those poor servants ; and promises him blessings for himself and for his children in this world and in the next, should he have full justice done to those who have been thus defrauded.

This, Sir, is the act of a good and virtuous slaveholder who feared God and promoted the best interests of religion, who was anxious to do justice and to show mercy to his slaves. This, Sir, was one of the greatest Popes that occupied the chair of St. Peter, a slaveholder whom the church venerates as one of her brightest examples of sanctity ; a saint, in honor of whom the present venerated pontiff selected the name which he bears, one who was well acquainted with his history, having studied it in the very monastery that he founded in the city of Rome, and over which the same Gregory XVI, presided, this latter was capable of distinguishing his sainted patron, a holder of slaves in domestic servitude, from the heartless and unjust man-stealer who makes the slave-trade his pursuit.

In the seventh book of his Epistles we find that marked 114, addressed to Brunichild, Queen of the Franks, and that numbered 115, to Theodoric and Theodobert, kings of the Franks, in which, amongst other requests, he entreats that they would prevent the Christians being held in slavery by the Jews. This was perhaps at the time required by the circumstances of the place and of the period, but certainly at the present time in this place, I know of no owners who treat their Catholic slaves with more kindness and affection, or who give them better opportunities for the practice of their religious duties, than do the Jewish owners. I have frequently found Catholic owners, who in this latter respect, are far behind the Jews, and who instead of giving to their servants good example and facilities and encouragement to be good Christians, faithful to their God and to their consciences, and conforming to the laws of the church, are the worst obstacles to their salvation.

In the fifth book of Epistles.—Ep. 36, to Columbus, bishop of Numidia, he complains grievously of the crime of those who allowed their children or their slaves to be baptized by the Donatist heretics,—and desires that any who should thereafter be guilty thereof should be excommunicated.

In his sixth book, Ep. 21, he commands the priest Candidus who was his agent in Gaul, to purchase four of the brothers of one Dominic, who complained to him that they were redeemed from their captors by Jews in Narbonne, and held by them in slavery.

Book third, Ep. 28, is a letter to Candidus, ordering a yearly pension to Albinus, a blind son of Martin, one of the colonists.

The seventh book, Ep. 22, to John, the bishop of Syracuse, is a very curious document. It recites the case of one Felix who was, it would seem, a slave born of Christian parents and given in his youth as a present to a Jew by a Christian owner; he served illegally during nineteen years the Jew who was disqualified from holding a Christian slave, but Maximinian the former bishop of Syracuse, learning the facts, had, as in duty bound, Felix discharged from this service and made free. Five years subsequently, a son of the Jew became, or pretended to become, a Christian, and being thus qualified to hold a Christian slave, claimed Felix as his property. Felix appealed to the Pope, and the letter to the bishop of Syracuse is a decision in favor of his freedom, containing also an order to the bishop to protect him and defend his liberty.

I believe, I may now safely dismiss Pope St. Gregory and pass over a mass of testimony on the subject, at least twice as large as that which I have adduced. He died in the year 604 of the Christian era: and thus we can perceive what was, during these six first ages of the Church, the doctrine and discipline regarding slavery.

I shall now, Sir, proceed with more celerity through several documents for subsequent ages.

I have the honor to be, sir,

Respectfully, &c.

† John, *Bishop of Charleston.*

Charleston, S. C., *February* 3, 1841.

LETTER XIV.

To the Hon. JOHN FORSYTH, Secretary of State, U. S.

Sir—Soon after the death of the holy Pope St. Gregory the Great, from whose writings I have made such copious extracts, an occurrence took place, which though it had no immediate bearing on the condition of slavery, yet, in its consequences through successive centuries, had a powerful and extensive influence upon that state. This was the innovation of Mahomet in Arabia. We shall, however, have to review many canons and other documents, before we shall have the Saracen or the Turk upon the field.

At the period to which we have arrived, the Lombards had the principal dominion in Italy; the Franks had obtained possession of the greater portion of ancient Gaul; the Goths had the dominion of Spain; Portugal was become an inheritance for the Suevi; Germany and the northern regions were filled by various hordes, who under several chiefs, were showing the first symptoms of civilization. England, under its Heptarchy, was imbibing from Augustine, the legate of St. Gregory, the religion which she for so many subsequent ages preserved; as yet, her common law had not even its foundations laid; and centuries were to elapse before Runnymede was to witness the delivery of *Magna Charta*: in the course of these times her Alfred and her Edward the Confessor were to appear. Wales contained the ancient British who had given way to the Anglo-Saxon; the Pict and the Scot occupied the northern plains and the snow-capped mountain; whilst Erin, with her Milesian progeny, cultivated literature and religion, as yet unassailed by the piratical Dane; Phocas wielded the sceptre of the East; Chosroes II, of the Parthian Dynasty, reigned in Persia, and Mahomet had as yet scarcely retired to concoct his mighty imposture in the cave of Hira; the Visigoth, the Vandal and the Moor spread themselves over the northern shores of Africa.

Look where you may, sir, through this map, the stain of slavery was upon every spot, and yet Christianity had already had six centuries of existence, and was, more or less powerfully, in possession of this wide domain. She had proclaimed mercy and charity, she had pronounced censures against the piratical invader, she had denounced the manstealer, she had inculcated obedience as the duty of the slave, kindness and protection as the obligation of the owner, and she had legislated for the direction of both. Could there be a more clear and unequivocal recognition of the lawfulness of holding property in the domestic slave ? I now proceed with the history of ecclesiastical legislation on the subject.

In the precept of king Clotaire II, for endowing the abbey of Corbey, after the grant of the parcels of land therein recited, he adds, " una cum terris domibus, mancipiis, ædificiis, vineis, silvis, pratis, pascuis, farinariis, et cunctis appenditiis," &c.—*Together with the lands, houses, slaves, buildings, vineyards, woods, meadows, pastures, granaries and all appendages.*

And the abbey not only possessed the slaves as property, but by the same precept had civil jurisdiction over all its territory and all persons and things thereon, to the exclusion of all other judges. Clotaire II died in 628.

The fourth Council of Toledo, in 633, in its 59th Canon, by the authority of king Sisenand and his nobles, &c., in Spain, restored to liberty any slaves whom the Jews should circumcise, and in the 66th canon, by the same authority, Jews were thenceforth rendered incapable of holding Christian slaves. The 70th and the 71st canons regulated the process regarding the freed persons and colonists of the church, and the latter affixed a penalty of reduction to slavery for some neglect of formal observances useful to preserve the evidence of title for the colonist. The 72d Canon places the freed persons, whether wholly manumitted or only conditioned, when settled under patronage of the church, under the protection of the clergy.

The 73d permits the ordination of persons fully manumitted by laics, but not of those liable to any condition.

The 74th allows the church to manumit worthy slaves belonging to herself, so that they may be ordained priests or deacons, but still keeps the property they may acquire, as belonging to the church which manumitted them, and restricts them even in their capacity as witnesses in several instances ; and should they violate this condition, declares them suspended.

In the year 650, which was the 6th of king Clovis II, a council was held at Chalons on the Saone in France, in whose ninth canon we perceive the dawning of that principle which thenceforth was, for a time, gradually to increase. The canon begins with the announcement of the principle.

" Pietatis est maximæ et religionis intuitus, ut captivitatis vinculum omnino à Christianis redimatur. Unde sancta synodus noscitur censuisse, ut nullus mancipium extra fines vel terminos qui ad regnum domini Clodovei regis pertinent, penitus, debeat venumdare ; ne quod absit per tale commercium aut captivitatis vinculo, vel quod pejus est, Judaicâ servitute mancipia Christiana teneantur implicita."

" It is a work of the greatest piety, and the intent of religion, that the bond of captivity should be entirely redeemed from Christians. Whence it is known to be the opinion of the holy synod, that no one ought, at all, to sell a slave beyond the dominions of our lord Clovis the king; lest, which God forbid, Christian slaves should be kept entangled in the chains of captivity, or what is worse, under Jewish bondage."

Thus, sir, after ages of confusion, invasion, civil war, strife and barbarity, the mild influence of religion had enlightened the minds and began to soften the hearts of that portion of the northern horde that occupied the fertile banks of the southern rivers of the ancient Gauls.

In the tenth Council of Toledo, celebrated in 656, in the reign of Receswind, king of the Goths, the 7th chapter is a bitter complaint of the practice which still prevailed amongst Christians, of selling Christian slaves to the Jews, to the subversion of their faith or their grievous oppression. And the council is the more afflicted at the enormous evil that priests and deacons, led away by avarice, and regardless of spiritual evils, were as deeply involved as lay persons in this criminal abuse. After a long and eloquent exposition of the evils which it produced, and ample quotation from holy writ, it concludes by pronouncing an excommunication, to be incurred by the fact, against all of any grade who shall thenceforth be thus criminal.

In the year 666, a council was held in Merida, in Spain. The 18th canon of which allows that, of the slaves belonging to the church, some may be ordained minor clerks, who shall serve the priests as their masters with due fidelity, receiving only food and raiment.

The twentieth chapter complains of many irregularities in the mode of making freed men for the service of the church, regulates the mode of making them, provides for the preservation of the evidence of their obligation and the security of their service.

The twenty-first regulates the extent to which a bishop shall be allowed to grant gifts to his friends, the slaves, the freed men, or others.

The thirteenth council of Toledo was held in 683, in the reign of Ervigius, the successor of Wamba. There was an old law of the Goths found in lib. v, tit. vii, and repeated in other forms in lib. 10 and 11, regulating that no freed man should do an injury or an unkindness to his master, and authorising the master who had suffered, to bring such offender back again to his state of slavery. And in lib. 17, the freed man and his progeny for ever, were prohibited from contracting marriage with the family of their patron or behaving with insolence to them. King Evigius was reminded by many of his nobles, that former kings in derogation of this law, had given employments about the palace to slaves and to freed men, and even sustained them in giving offence to their masters, had even sometimes ordered them so to do, and protected them; for this the nobles sought redress. The king called upon the council to unite with him in putting a stop to this indignity. And in the sixth canon we have the detail of the evils set forth, and also the enactment, in concurrence with the king, that thenceforward it shall be unlawful to give any employment whatever about the palace, or in the concerns of the crown, to any freed men or slaves, but to those belonging to the fisc, and punishes the attempt of the slave or freed man who may transgress or offend, with correction, or even reduction to slavery, if he be not a slave.

The third council of Saragossa was celebrated in the year 691, in the reign of Egica, king of the Goths.

It will be recollected that in previous councils in Spain, especially in some of Toledo, it had been enacted, that any freed man of the church, who did not comply with certain regulations, should lose his freedom and be reduced to slavery. One of the conditions was, that any person pretending to have been manumitted or claiming as the descendant of a freed man, should, upon the death of the bishop, exhibit his papers to the successor of the deceased, within a year, or upon his neglect, should be declared a slave. The object of this was to discern those who were really partially free from the perfect slave, and to cause the former to preserve their muniments.

The fathers of Saragossa, however, discovered that, as they express it, some of the bishops, studying their own gain, had been too rigid in enforcing this law, and thereby reduced several negligent or ignorant persons to bondage ; in order then to do justice, they enacted in their fourth chapter, that the year within which the documents should be exhibited, should not commence to run until after the new bishop, subsequently to his institution, should have given sufficient notice to those claiming to be but in partial service, to produce their papers.

The sixteenth council of Toledo, in Spain, was held in the year 693. The fifth chapter of the acts relates to the repairs of churches, and after referring to the ancient canons regulating that when the bishop received the third of the revenue of the parish, he was bound to repair the church, and determining when a priest may hold two churches, it has the following passage.

" Ut ecclesia, quæ usque ad decem habuerit mancipia, super se habeat sacerdotem, quæ vero minus decem mancipia habuerit aliis conjungatur ecclesiis."

" That the church which shall have as many as ten slaves, shall have one priest over it, but that one which shall have less than ten slaves shall be united to other churches."

Though I can scarcely find an instance at this period where the word *mancipium* is used for land, yet, as the word has frequently been used in that sense, it may possibly be its meaning in this place. The whole tenor however, of the Spanish canons during the dominion of the Visigoths, exhibits the churches as in possession of slaves equally as of lands, and indeed throughout the centuries that we now examine, land would have been about as valuable without slaves, in Spain, as it would be this day in Georgia.

In the tenth chapter of the acts of the same council, not only was excommunication pronounced against all who should be guilty of high treason against Egica, the king of the Gothic nation, but the bishops and clergy united with the nobles (palatii senioribus) and the popular representatives in condemning traitors and their progeny to perpetual slavery (fisci viribus sub perpetuâ servitute maneant religati.)

It may not be amiss to add to the above a couple of the laws of Ina, king of the West Saxons or Wessex, or about the year 692. They were made for the regulation of religion.

III.—" Servus, si quid operis patrarit die dominico, ex præcepto domini sui, liber esto, dominus triginta solidos dependito. Verum si id operis injussu domini sui aggressus fuerit, verberibus cæditor, aut saltem virgarum metum precio redimito. Liber, si die hoc operetur injussu domini sui, aut servituti addicitor, aut sexaginta solidos dependito. Sacerdos, si in hanc partem deliquerit, pœna in duplum augeator."

" If a slave shall do any work on the Lord's day, by order of his master, let him become free, and let the master pay thirty shillings (another copy adds, ' ad Witam,' as a fine.) But, if he went to this work without his master's command, let him be cut with whips, (another copy has ' corium perdat,' let him lose his skin,) or at least, let him redeem the fear of the scourge by a price. A freeman, if on this day he shall work without the order of his lord, let him be reduced to slavery, or pay sixty shillings. Should a priest be delinquent in this respect, his penalty shall be increased to double."

The sixth regards broils and quarrels. One of the clauses is, that whosoever shall fight in the dwelling of a villain or colonist, shall pay his year's rent or thirty shillings to the villain.

In the eighth, the division of the weregild for the killing of a stranger, between the king and the family of the deceased is fixed, as also the share of an abbot or of an abbess, if either of them had special rights. We have then the following passage :—

" Wallus censum pendens annuum, 120 solidorum æstimatur, filius cjus, 100. Servus, alias 60, alias 50, solidis valere putatur. Wallus virgarum metum 12 solidis redimito. Wallus quinque terræ hydas possidens 600 solidis æstimandus est."

"A stranger paying a yearly rent, is to be rated at 120 shillings, his son at 100. A slave at either 50 or 60, is a fair estimation. Let a stranger redeem his fear of whipping for 12 shillings. A stranger being in possession of five hydes of land is to be valued at 600 shillings.

The Anglo-Saxons were very much disposed to treat strangers with contempt: their usual phrase for "a stranger was *Walea*, or Latin, "Wallus." Silvester Giradus, in his *Descriptio Cambriæ, cap. 7.*

When the Anglo-Saxons got into possession of the chief part of Britain, the ancient British were called " Walli," or strangers, and hence the place to which they retreated was called Wealas, or Wales, to which the Normans subsequently gave the name of *Pays des Galles*. The Irish used to call foreigners, *Gaul*. Thus by the laws of Ina, the Welshman was worth twice as much as a slave, for his Weregild, but if he possessed five hydes of land, he was rated at ten or twelve times the Weregild of the slave. This is in the law xxii, of Ina, in the general compilation, but selecting from the ecclesiastical it is No. viii.

The seventeenth council of Toledo was celebrated in 694, in the reign of the same Egica. A sentence appended to it regards what I should hope had ceased to be a custom long before this period, but was, as I have before observed, enacted at Agde and at Epao, long previous to this. There were twenty-three of these sentences, the fifteenth of which is :

" Si quis servum proprium sine conscientiâ judicis occiderit, excommunicatione biennii sanguinis se mundabit."

" If any one shall put his own slave to death, without the knowledge of the judge, he shall cleanse himself the blood by an excommunication of two years."

In the Council of Berghamstead, near Canterbury, held in 697, under Withred, king of Kent, at which Gebmund, bishop of Rochester, was present, and where a sort of Parliament also assembled and gave a civil sanction to the temporal enactments and penalties of the Canons, several regulations were made concerning slaves. The Saxon MS, is the adoption of the canons into the common law of Canterbury, and is entitled " *The Judgments of Withred*."

The ninth Canon in this collection is the following:

" Si quis servum suum ad altare manumiserit, liber esto, et habilis sit ad gaudendum hereditate et wirigildo, et fas sit ei ubi volet sine limite versari."

" If any person shall manumit his servant at the altar, let him be free, and capable of enjoying inheritance and weregild, and let it be lawful for him to dwell where he pleases without limit."

The tenth Canon is:

" Si in vesperâ præcedente diem solis postquam sol occubuit, aut in vesperâ præcedente diem lunæ post occasum solis servus ex mandato domini sui opus aliquod servile egerit, dominus factum octoginta solidis luito."

" If on the evening preceding Sunday, after the sun has set, or on the evening preceding Monday, after the setting of the sun, a slave shall do any servile work by command of his master, let the master compensate the deed by eighty shillings."

The eleventh:

" Si servus hisce diebus itineraverit, domino pendat sex solidos, aut flagello cœdatur."

" If a servant shall have journeyed on these days, let him pay six shillings to his master, or be cut with a whip."

The twelfth:

" Si liber homo [id faciat] tempore vetito, sit reus collistrigii mulctæ: et qui eum detulerit, dimidium habeat tam mulctæ quam wirgildi."

" If a freeman [shall do so] on a forbidden time, let him be liable to the fine of the pillory: and let the informer have one-half as well of the fine as of the weregild."

The thirteenth:

" Si paganus uxore nesciâ diabolo quid obtulerit, omnibus fortunis suis plectatur et collistrigio. Sin et ambo pariter itidem fecerint, omnium honorum suorum amissione, ipsa etiam luat et collistrigio."

" If a villain, without the knowledge of his wife, shall have offered any thing to the devil, let him be punished by the loss of all his fortune and by the pillory. And if both did so together, let her also lose all her goods and be punished by the pillory."

I need not inform you, sir, that the English *villain* was the *colonist* of the European continent, and that in the Speculum Saxonicum, lib. 1, art. 3, you will find the description of his imperfect liberty as compared with the free man. You will also find it in Du Cange.—Paganus Pagenses, &c.

The fourteenth:

" Si servus diabolo offerat, sex dependat solidos, aut flagro vapulet."

" If a slave offers to the devil, let him pay six shillings or be whipped."

The fifteenth:

" Si quis servo carnem in jejunio dederit comedendam, servus liber exeat."

"If any one shall give his slave flesh-meat to eat on a fast day, let the slave go out free."

The sixteenth:

"Si servus ex sponte suâ eam ederit, aut sex solidis aut flagello."

"If the slave shall eat it of his own motion, let the penalty be either six shillings or a whipping."

After regulating the mode of declaration of swearing and of compurgation, for the king, the bishop, the abbot, the priest, the deacon, the cleric, the stranger, and the king's thane, the twenty-first canon enacts:

"Paganus cum quatuor compurgatoribus, capite suo ad altare inclinato, semet eximat."

"Let the villain deliver himself with four compurgators, with his head bowed down to the altar."

The twenty-third:

"Si quis Dei mancipium in conventu suo accusaverit, dominus ejus eum simplici suo juramento purgabit, si eucharistiam susceperit. Ad eucharistiam autem si nusquam venerit, habeat in juramento fidejussorem bonum, vel solvat, vel se tradat flagellandum."

"If any person shall accuse a slave of God in his convent, his lord shall purge him with a simple oath if he shall have received the eucharist. But if he has never come to the eucharist, let him in his oath have a good surety to answer, or let him pay or give himself up to be whipped."

The slave of God was one belonging to a monastery, of whom there appear to have been a good number in England, at that period, as well as on the continent. The previous canon had legislated for the bishop's dependants as distinguished from the slave of the monastery.

The twenty-fourth canon is:

"Si servus viri popularis servum viri ecclesiastici accusaverit, vel servus ecclesiastici servum viri popularis, dominus ejus singulari suo juramento eum expurgabit."

"If the slave of a lay person shall accuse the slave of a clergyman, or if the slave of a clergyman shall accuse the slave of a layman, let his master purge him by his single oath."

The twenty-sixth canon regulated the punishment of a freeman who was detected carrying away what he had stolen.

The twenty-seventh regulated the punishment of the person who permitted a thievish slave to escape, and respecting the slave himself concluded thus:

"Si quis eum occiderit, domino ejus dimidium pendito."

"If any one shall slay him, let him pay to his master one half."

In Germany, however, as yet, in most places, paganism prevailed, and human sacrifices were offered. St. Boniface had been sent by the Holy See, to endeavor to reclaim to religion and to civilization the nations or tribes that composed this undefined extent of territory. We find in a letter of Pope Gregory III, written in answer to his request for special instructions about the year 735, the following paragraph:

" Hæc quoque inter alia crimina agi in partibus illis dixisti, quod quidem ex fidelibus ad immolandum paganis sua venumdent mancipia. Quod ut magnopere corrigere debeas frater, commonemus, nec sinas fieri ultra: scelus est enim et impietas. Eis ergo qui hæc perpetraverunt, similem homicidæ indices pænitentiam."

" You have said that amongst other crimes this was done in those parts, that some of the faithful sold their slaves to pagans to be immolated. Which you should use all your power to correct, nor allow it to be done any more: for it is wickedness and impiety. Impose then upon its perpetrators the same penance as for homicide."

This exhibition, sir, brings us over another century of the view, which I proposed to take.

I have the honor to be, sir,
Respectfully, &c.
† JOHN, Bishop of Charleston.

CHARLESTON, S. C., <i>Feb.</i> 11, 1841.

<hr>

LETTER XV.

To THE HON JOHN FORSYTH, SECRETARY OF STATE, U. S.

SIR,—I proceed with the history of ecclesiastical legislation concerning slaves. My last letter brought us up to the year 735. I shall, however, before proceeding forward, introduce a small portion of an earlier document.

I omitted to introduce in its proper order the testimony of Theodore, archbishop of Canterbury, who died in the year 690, and in whose capitulary we find the concurrent testimony of the east and of the west, as he was a native of Tarsus, in Cilicia, the city of St. Paul. He dwelt for some years in Rome, and then governed the English church for upwards of twenty years. I shall make a few extracts from his canonical regulations.

" VII. Græci et Romani dant servis suis vestimenta, et laborant excepto Dominico die. Græcorum monachi servos non habent, Romani habent."

" The Greeks and Romans give clothing to their slaves, and they work except on the Lord's day. The Greek monks have not slaves, the Romans have."

" XVII. Ingenuus cum ingenuâ conjungi debet."

" A free man should be married to a free woman."

" LXV. Qui per jussionem domini sui occiderit hominem, dies xl, jejunet."

" He who, by the command of his master, shall kill a man shall fast forty days."

The 71st prohibits the intermarriages of those slaves whose owners will prevent their living together.

The 74th regulates that if a free pregnant woman be sold into slavery, the child that she bears shall be free; all subsequently born shall be slaves.

" LXXIX. Pater filium necessitate coactus in servitium sine voluntate filii tradat."

" A father, compelled by necessity, may deliver his son into slavery without the will of that son."

" LXXXIX. Episcopus et abbas hominem sceleratum servum possunt habere, si precium redimendi non habet."

"A bishop or an abbot can hold a criminal in slavery, if he have not the price of his redemption."

" CXVII. Servo pecuniam per laborem comparatam nulli licet auferre."

" It is not lawful for any one to take away from a slave the money made by labor."

I shall pass over a number of acts which only renewed or remodelled the provisions that we have previously seen, and I come to the year 752. In this year Pepin, son of Charles Martel, mayor of the palace, and father of Charlemagne, got possession of the throne of France, was crowned at Soissons by St. Boniface, archbishop of Mayence, and thus founded the second dynasty of the French monarchy. One of his earliest acts was to call an assembly of the French nobles and bishops. They met at Vermeria, now called Verberie, in the department of Oise. The prelates held a council, at which twenty-one canons were made, a few of which will exhibit to us the legislation of that period regarding slaves.

Perhaps it may be as well here to observe that about this period it was usual to hold such joint meetings, and it frequently happened that the bishops also profited of their occasion for holding their own councils; hence, when the acts of the general assembly and those of the council

were copied, it not unfrequently happened that the canons on ecclesiastical affairs were found on the same record with civil and political statutes
and regulations. Thus it not unfrequently happened also that civil laws
were found on the rolls of canonical proceedings. And, looking at the
records of this and the five or six succeeding centuries, the careless or
the uninformed reader may be led to conclude that acts which were never
treated of in ecclesiastical councils, were the legislation of the church,
and also that lay or mixed assemblies had enacted canons for the regulation of religion. It must however be observed that it also frequently
happened that the same subject was treated of in each assembly, but under different relations; in the one as it regarded the doctrine or discipline
of the church, in the other as it regarded the concerns of the state; and
the two enactments were not always separately engrossed. I will not
however deny that during this period usurpations of power were occasionally attempted, on both sides, and not always without success.

In this council of Verberie, which was held in a palace of King Pepin,
the sixth canon made regulations in the case of marriage between free
persons and slaves. The following are its provisions:

1. If any free person contracted marriage with a slave, being at the
time ignorant of the state of bondage of that party, the marriage was invalid.

2. If a person under bond should have a semblance of freedom by reason of condition, and the free person be ignorant of the bondage, and this
bond person should be brought into servitude, the marriage was declared
originally void.

3. An exception was made where the bond person, by reason of want,
should with the consent of the free party, sell himself or herself into perfect slavery with the consent of the free party, then the marriage was to
stand good, because the free party had consented to the enslavement, and
profited of its gains.

The seventh canon would seem to show us that a slave could hold property in slaves; but probably the *servus* there described was a *conditiona-
tus*, or person held to certain services, and not a *mancipium*, or absolute
slave.

" Si servus suam ancillam concubinam habuerit, si ita placet, potest illâ
dimissâ comparem suam ancillam domini sui accipere: sed melius est
suam ancillam tenere."

" If a man servant shall have his own female slave as a concubine, he
shall have power, if he wishes, leaving her, to marry his equal, the female
servant of his master: but it is better that he should keep his own servant
in wedlock."

The eighth canon provided, in the case of a freedman who, subsequently to his liberation, committed sin with the female slave of his former master, that the master should have power, whether the freedman would or not, to compel him to marry that female slave ; and should this man leave her, and attempt a marriage with another woman, this latter must be separated from him.

The thirteenth declares that when a freeman, knowing that the woman whom he is about to marry is a slave, or not having known it until after marriage, voluntarily upon the discovery consents to the marriage, it is thenceforth indissoluble.

The nineteenth declares that the separation of married parties, by the sale of one who is a slave, does not affect the marriage. They must be admonished, if they cannot be reunited, to remain continent.

The twentieth provides for the case of a male slave freed by letter (*chartellarius*), who having for his wife taken a slave with the lawful consent of her master, and, leaving her, takes another as his wife. The latter contract is void, and the parties must separate.

Another assembly was held by King Pepin, in Compeigne, forty-eight miles north-east of Paris, where he had a country seat. At this assembly also the prelates held a council in 757, and made eighteen canons. The fourth makes provision for the case of a man's giving his free step-daughter, that is, the daughter of his wife by a previous marriage, in wedlock to a freeman or to a slave. The fifth declares void the marriage between a free person and a slave, where the former was ignorant of the condition of the latter. The sixth regards a case of a complicated description, where a freeman got a civil benefice from his lord, and takes his own vassal with him, and dies upon the benefice, leaving after him the vassal. Another freeman becomes invested with the benefice, and, anxious to induce the vassal to remain, gives him a female serf attached to the soil as his wife. Having lived with her for a time, the vassal leaves her, and returns to the lord's family, to which he owed his services, and there he contracts a marriage with one of the same allegiance. His first contract was invalid, the second was the marriage.

In the year 772 a council was held in Bavaria, at a place called *Dingolvinga* (which, as far as I can discover by comparison of maps and similarity of name, is the present city of Ingolstadt), in the reign of Tassilo, duke of Bavaria. The tenth canon of this council decides that a noble woman, who had contracted marriage with a slave, not being aware of his condition, is at liberty to leave him, the contract being void, and she is to be considered free and not to be reduced to slavery. By *noble* we are here to understand *free*, as distinguished from *ignoble*, that is, a slave.

To understand the full bearing of some parts of this canon, it is necessary to know what the laws of Bavaria at that time regulated concerning
free women who married slaves.   And we find sufficient for our purpose
upon the record of the assembly which was held for the purpose of civil
legislation, at the same period that this council was celebrated.   It recites,
after giving the fourteen canons of the council, that under the everlasting
reign of our Lord Jesus Christ, but in the 22d year of the most religious
Tassilo, duke of the Bojoari, on the 11th of the ides of October, in the
year of the incarnation of our Lord 772, the tenth indiction, the aforesaid prince held an assembly at Dingolvinga, a public town, where he had
gathered his chiefs.   And a monastery of men, as also one of females,
having been there founded, and the bishops having made their canons, the
laws of the nation were revised by the consent of the skilful chiefs and of
all the assembly.   We have then sixteen amendments of the national law.

The first regulates by the authority of the prince and consent of the
whole assembly, that thenceforth no slave, whether fugitive or other,
should be sold beyond the limits of the territory under penalty of the payment of his weregild.

In the second, among other things, it is enacted that if a slave should
be killed in the commission of house-breaking, his owner is to receive no
compensation; and should the felon who is killed in man-stealing, when
he could not be taken, whether it be a freeman or a slave that he is carrying off, no weregild shall be paid by the slayer, but he shall be bound to
prove his case before a court.

The seventh regards the trial by ordeal of slaves freed by the duke's
hand.

The eighth establishes and guards the freedom not only of themselves,
but of their posterity, for those freed in the church, unless when they may
be reduced to slavery from inability to pay for damages which they had
committed.

The ninth contains, amongst other enactments, those which explain the
tenth canon of the council.   After specifying different weregilds for freed
persons, it says:

"Si ancilla libera dimissa fuerit per chartam aut in ecclesiâ, et post
hæc servo nupserit, ecclesiæ ancilla permanebit."

"Should a female slave be emancipated by deed or in the church, and
afterwards marry a slave, she shall be a slave to the church."

It then continues respecting a woman originally free, and, as I suppose,
the *nobilis* of canon x.

"Si autem libera Bajoaria servo Ecclesiæ nupserit, et servile opus ancilla contradixerit, abscedat."

" But if a free Bavarian female shall have married a servant of the church, and the maid will not submit to servile work, she may depart."

I suppose from the subsequent portion of the law, as well as from the Christian doctrine of the indissolubility of a perfect marriage, that in this case there was merely a contract, not followed by its consummation; for the law proceeds:

" Si autem ibi filios et filias generavērit, ipsi servi et ancillæ permaneant, potestatem exinde (exeundi) non habeant."

" But if she shall have there borne sons and daughters, they shall continue slaves, and not have power of going forth."

Her freedom was not however immediately destroyed, for the law proceeds:

" Illa autem mater eorum, quando exire voluerit, ante annos iii, liberam habeat potestatem."

" But she, their mother, when she may desire to go forth before three years, shall have free power therefor."

In this case the marriage subsisted, but the free woman could separate, without however the marriage bond being rent. If she remained beyond the time of three years, she lost her freedom; and it shows us that, probably previous to this amendment, any free woman who married a slave, thereby lost her own freedom; and that the tenth canon, showing the marriage of which it treated to be invalid, showed that the woman should not lose her liberty. The concluding provision of the ninth law is as follows:

" Si autem iii annos induraverit opus ancillæ et parentes ejus non exadomaverunt eam ut libera fuisset, nec ante comitem ducem, nec ante regem nec in publico mallo, transactis tribus kalendis Martis (Martu), post hæc ancilla permaneat in perpetuum et quicumque ex ea nati fuerint servi et ancillæ sunt."

" But if she shall have continued three years doing the work of a slave, and her relations have not brought her out so that she should be free, either before the count, or the duke, or the king, or in the public high court (mall), when the kalends of March shall have thrice passed, after this she shall remain perpetually a slave, and they who shall be born of her, male and female, shall be slaves.

In 768 Charlemagne succeeded Pepin in the rule of one portion of his dominions, and three years afterwards, upon the death of his brother Carloman, he succeeded to the remainder. This is not the place to give his history, but I merely remark that in the collection of canon law taken from the various councils for the preceding centuries, and then in force, which was delivered to him by Pope Adrian I, in the year 774, we find

nearly all those which I have previously adverted to, or quoted, respecting slaves. I shall instance a few: the 3d of Gangræ, condemning as
guilty of heresy those who taught that religion sanctioned the slave in
despising his master ; the 30th in the African collection, which showed
that the power of manumission in the church was derived from the civil
authority : the 102d of the same, which declared slaves and freed persons
disqualified to prosecute, except in certain cases and for injuries done to
themselves.

In a capitulary of Charlemagne, published in such a synod and general
assembly in 779, in the month of March, in the eleventh year of his reign,
at Duren, on the Roer (Villa Duria), between Cologne and Aix-la-Chapelle, there being assembled "episcopis, abbatibus, virisque illustribus
comitibus, unâ cum piissimo domino nostro,"—the bishops, abbots, and
the illustrious men, the counts, together with our most pious lord, we find
the following chapter :

"XX. De mancipiis quæ venduntur, ut in præsentiâ episcopi vel comitis sit, aut in præsentiâ archdiaconi, aut centenarii, aut in præsentiâ vice-
domini, aut judicis comitis, aut ante bene nota testimonia. Et foras
marcham, nemo mancipium vendat. Qui fecerit, tantis vicibus bannos
solvet, quanta mancipia vendidit. Et si non habet precium vivadio, pro
servo semetipsum donet comiti, usquèdum ipsos bannos solvat."

"Concerning slaves that are sold, let it be in presence of the bishop,
or of the count, or in presence of the archdeacon, or of the judge of the
hundred, or in presence of the lord's deputy, or of the judge of the county,
or of well known witnesses. And let no one sell a slave beyond the
boundary. Whosoever shall do so shall pay as many fines as he sold
slaves. And if he has not the money, let him deliver himself to the count
in pledge as a slave until he shall pay the fines."

The bishops and abbots were concurring parties to this chapter, and
Charlemagne was a good practical religious man.

In a capitulary of Pope Adrian I, containing the summary of the chief
part of the canon law then in force as collected from the ancient councils
and other sources, delivered to Ingilram, bishop of Metz, òr, as it was
then called, Divodurum, or oppidum Mediomatricorum, on the 19th of
September, xiii. kalendas Octobres, indic. ix, 785. The sixteenth chapter, describing those who cannot be witnesses against priests, mentions not
merely slaves, but "quorum vitæ libertas nescitur," those *who are not
known to be free;* and in the notes of Anthony Augustus, bishop of Tar-
ragona, on this capitulary, he refers for this and another passage, "viles
personæ"—*persons of vile condition,* which is the appellation of slaves, to
decrees of the earliest of popes, viz., Anacletus, A. D. 91, and Clement,

his immediate successor; Evaristus, who was the next, and died A. D. 109; Pius, who died A. D. 157; Calistus, in 222; Fabian, 250; and several others. In chapter xxi, among incompetent witnesses, are recited, " nullus servus, nullus libertus"—*no slave, no freedman.* The notes of the same author inform us that this portion of the chapter is the copy of an extract from the first council of Nice, and that it is also substantially found in a passage from Pope Pontianus, who died in 235, as well in several of the early African and Spanish councils which he quotes.

I have already noticed the collection of canon law given by Pope Adrian to Charlemagne. That monarch having the best possible understanding with the holy see, animated by an ardent zeal for the progress of religion and the establishment of morality, was also one of the most active and indefatigable princes, a profound statesman, and a skilful and successful general.

He assembled many councils of prelates, nobles, and other advisers, and having all the topics on which he determined to legislate maturely discussed by each order of persons, in its proper place, he embodied into enactments, called Capitularies, the legislative results. We have several of these ; a large portion of them are chapters, or *capita*, making the canons and the decisions which he received from the pope, the law of the kingdom, and subsequently, when he had been crowned emperor, the law of the empire. In most of the chapters reference is made to the council which enacted the provision, and to the canon in which the enactment is found, and frequently the very words of the canon are used. It was thus that a large portion of the canon law became the public law of the greater part of Europe, by civil legislation, and not by papal encroachment ; and it exhibits either very imperfect knowledge or great dishonesty in a large number of writers upon law, especially of the English and American schools, when at this day they continue to retail the falsehoods and calumnies of earlier historians, who, to subserve the purposes of innovators, have falsified history.

I am indeed disposed to make great allowance for our American writers, not one in twenty of whom, perhaps, ever laid his eye upon one of the documents of which I treat, and who takes for granted all that an English jurist or a European infidel writes upon the subject.

One of these assemblies in which Charlemagne published a capitulary, was held at Aix-la-Chapelle (Aquisgranum) in 789, in which eighty-two chapters were enacted. No. xxiii is founded upon canon iv of the council of Chalcedon, and upon an enactment of Leo the great, the latter of which I have given in Letter VI, on the 4th of November. It prohibited all attempts to induce a slave to embrace either the clerical or monastical state, without the will and license of the master. No. xlv prohibits, amongst others, slaves from being competent witnesses, or freedmen against their patrons: founded upon the 96th canon of the African councils, quoted in Letter V, October 28th. No. lvii, referring to the 3d canon of the council of Gangræ, mentioned also in Letter V, prohibits bishops ordaining slaves without the master's license.

In 794 a council was held at Frankfort on the Maine, at which the bishops of a large portion of Europe assisted, the 23d canon of which is the following:

" De servis alienis, ut a nemine recipiantur, neque ab episcopis sacrentur sine licentiâ dominorum."

" Of servants belonging to others: they shall be received by no one, nor admitted to orders by bishops, without their masters' license."

In the year 697, at another assembly held at Aix-la-Chapelle, the capitulary for the pacification and government of Saxony was enacted by Charlemagne. The eighth chapter is:

" Si quis hominem diabolo sacrificaverit, et in hostiam more paganorum dæmonibus obtulerit, morte moriatur."

" If any person shall sacrifice a man to the devil, and offer him as a victim to devils after the fashion of pagans, he shall be put to death."

I beg, for an explanation of this, to refer to the concluding part of Letter XIV, February 11th, where Pope Gregory III answers St. Boniface, who informed him that unfortunate slaves were bought to be thus immolated.

" XI. Si quis filiam domini sui rapuerit, more moriatur."

" If any one shall do violence to his master's daughter, he shall be put to death."

" XII. Si quis dominum suum vel dominam suam interfecerit, simili modo puniatur."

" If any one shall kill his master or his mistress, he shall be punished in like manner."

" XIV. De minoribus capitulis consenserunt omnes, ad unamquemque ecclesiam curtem et duas mansas terræ pagenses ad ecclesiam recurrentes condonent: et inter centum viginti homines nobiles et ingenuos, similiter et litos, servum et ancillam eidem ecclesiæ tribuant."

" All agreed concerning the smaller congregations, that the colonists frequenting each church should bestow upon it one dwelling, with proper out offices, and two manses of land; and that they should give to the same church one male slave and one female slave between one hundred and twenty noble and free men, and counting also the conditioned servants."

Thus in this newly settled ecclesiastical province the provision made for the support of religion consisted of land and slaves; and the *liti*, or servants under condition, were to be counted as freemen in taking the census. The *mansa* was generally as much good land as could be tilled by a servile family and a pair of oxen, and was computed to be about twelve acres.

I had hoped in this letter to make progress through a large number of years, but I find the documents before me too numerous to press into the space that remains. I shall reserve them for my next.

I have the honor to be, sir,

Respectfully, &c.

† JOHN, *Bishop of Charleston.*

CHARLESTON, S. C., *January* 28, 1841.

LETTER XVI.

To THE HON. JOHN FORSYTH, SECRETARY OF STATE, U. S.

SIR,—I proceed with the capitularies of Charlemagne. He was crowned Emperor of the Romans on Christmas day, in the year 800, by Pope Leo III, at High Mass, in the church of the Vatican, before the confession of St. Peter, or the tomb where one-half of the body of that blessed apostle is laid up, together with one-half of that of St. Paul :—and thus was the Western empire re-established.

The Lombards had long disturbed Italy, Charlemagne succeeded in reducing them to better order, and in the year 801, he, by a capitulary, amended their laws. I shall exhibit one chapter by which the colonial state in Italy was assimilated to that of France and of Germany.

VI. *De aldionibus publicis ad jus publicum pertinentibus.*

" Aldiones vel aldianes eâ lege vivant in Italiâ, in servitute dominorum suorum, quâ fiscalini, vel liddi vivunt in Franciâ."

Of the public Aldions, belonging to the public estate.

" The Aldions, or Aldians, shall in Italy, exist upon the same principle in the service of their masters that the fiscals and lids do exist in France."

The Aldions were bonds-men or bonds-women, whose persons were not at the disposal of their masters, nor did they pass with the land as colonists did, but their masters or patrons had certain claims upon stated ser-

vices from them. They were generally either freed persons or the descendants of those who had been manumitted upon the condition of performing
stipulated services, and if they failed to perform these they were liable to
be reduced to slavery. The fisc was originally a basket or frail, into
which the common property was put, it was then a bag or sack, for holding money, and lastly came to mean the treasury, and by common use to
be generally confined to the *State* Treasury or monarch's treasury ; hence
the *fiscalini* or *fiscal servants* were, in France, persons who owed certain
fixed services to *the fisc* or treasury of the monarch, of the state, or of
some community, or church, or public body. The *Lidus* or *Liddus* or
litus of the Saxon was so called from being spared in the conquest, and
left on the land with the obligation of paying the master, who owned it and
himself, a certain portion of its produce, and doing him other fixed services. Thus neither of them was an absolute slave whose person and property were at the owner's disposal. The slave was manumitted, but this
latter description of servants were generally released by deed or charter :
hence, when so freed they were called *chartulani, chartellani*, or " char-
tered." The transition from slavery to this latter kind of servitude was
at the commencement of the ninth century greatly on the increase.

VIII. " *De servis fugacibus.*

" Ubique intra Italiam, sive regius, sive ecclesiasticus vel cujuslibet
alterius hominis servus fugitivus inventus fuerit à domino suo sine ullâ
annorum præscriptione vindicetur, eâ tamen ratione, si dominus Francus
sive Alemannus, aut alterius cujuslibet nationis sit. Si verò Longobardus
aut Romanus fuerit, eâ lege servos suos vel adquirat vel admittat, quæ
antiquitùs inter eos constitutus est."

" *Concerning runaway slaves.*

" Wheresoever within the bounds of Italy, either the runaway slave of
the king or of the church or of any other man, shall be found by his master, he shall be restored without any bar of prescription of years ;
yet upon the provision that the master be a Frank or a German or of any
other nation (foreign). But if he be a Lombard or a Roman, he shall
acquire or receive his slaves by that law which has been established from
ancient times amongst them."

Here again is abundant evidence of the prevalent usage of the church
holding property in slaves ; just as commonly as did the king or any other
person.

In the year 805, Charlemagne published a capitulary at Thionville, in
the department of Moselle, France, (Theodonis villa.) In the chap. xi,
we read :

" *De servis propriis vel ancillis.*

" De propriis servis et ancillis, ut non suprà modum in monasteria sumantur, ne deserentur villæ."

" *Concerning their own male or female slaves.*

" Let not an excessive number of their own male or female slaves be taken into the monasteries, lest the farms be deserted."

This capitulary regards principally the regulation of monasteries.

St. Pachomius, who was born in Upper Egypt, in 292, and who was the first that drew up a regular monastic rule, would never admit a slave into a monastery.—*Tillemont,* vii, p. 180.

In the year 813, a council was held at Chalons, on the Saone, in France, the portions of whose enactments in any way affecting property or civil rights were confirmed by Charlemagne and made a portion of the law of the empire.

Many of the churches, especially in the country, were curtailed in their income and reduced to difficulties, because the bishops and abbots had large estates within their parishes, and many servants occupied in their cultivation, and the prelates prevented these servants paying tythes to the parish clergy, claiming for themselves an exemption from the obligation. The canon xix is the following—

" Questi sunt præterèa quidam fratres, quod essent quidam episcopi et abbates, qui decimas non sinerent dari ecclesiis ubi illi coloni missas audiunt. Proinde decrevit sacer ille conventus, ut episcopi et abbates de agris et vineis, quæ ad suum vel fratrum stipendium habent, decimas ad ecclesias deferri faciant: familiæ vèro ibi dent decimas suas, ubi infantes eorum baptizantur, et ubi per totum anni circulum missas audiunt."

" Moreover some brethren have complained, that there were some bishops and abbots who would not permit tythes to be given to those churches where colonists hear mass. Wherefore that holy assembly decreed, that, for those fields and vineyards which they have for their own support or that of their brethren, the bishops and abbots should cause the tythe to be paid to the churches. And let the servants pay their tythes to 'the church where their infants are baptized and where during the year, they hear mass."

In this we have additional evidence, if it were wanted, of the fact that large bodies of land and numerous servants attached to them were held by bishops and abbots, not only for themselves, but for their churches and their monasteries. The canon xxx, is the following—

" Dictum nobis est quod quidam legitima servorum matrimonia potestativâ quâdam præsumptione dirimant, non attendentes illud evangelicum : *Quod Deus conjunxit, homo non separet.* Unde nobis visum est, ut conjugia servorum non dirimantur, etiam si diversos dominos habeant : sed in uno conjugio permanentes dominis suis serviant. Et hoc in illis observandum est, ubi legalis conjunctio fuit, et per voluntatem dominorum."

"It has been stated to us that some persons, by a sort of magisterial presumption, dissolve the lawful marriages of slaves ; not regarding that evangelical maxim, *What God hath put together, let man not separate.* Whence it appears to us, that the wedlock of slaves may not be dissolved even though they have different masters ; but let them serve their masters remaining in one wedlock. And this is to be observed with regard to those where there has been a lawful union, and with the will of the owners."

Charlemagne died in the year 814, and was succeeded in the empire by Louis the weak, or the pious. In the third year of his reign, in the year 816, a council was held at Aix-la-Chapelle, in which a large portion of the canon law then in force regarding the clergy was embodied into 145 chapters. After the session of the council, the emperor published a capitulary containing thirty chapters ; the sixth of which complains of the continued indiscretion of bishops in ordaining servants, contrary to the canons, and forbids such ordinations except upon the master's giving full liberty to the slave : declares also, that if a servant shall impose upon a bishop by false witnesses or documents of freedom, and thus procure ordination, he shall be deposed and taken back by his owner. If the descendant of a slave who came from abroad, shall have been educated and ordained, where there was no knowledge of his condition, should his owner subsequently discover him and prove his property, if this owner grants him liberty he may keep his clerical rank ; but if the master asserts his right and carries him away, though the slave does not lose his character of order, he loses his rank and cannot officiate. Should masters give servants freedom that they may be capable of ordination, it shall be in the masters' discretion to give or to withhold the property necessary to enable the person to get orders.

The archbishops are to have in each province the emperor's authority in the original, to authorize their ordaining the servants of the church, and the suffragan bishops are to have copies of this original, and when such servant is to be ordained, this authority must be read for the people from the pulpit or at the corner of the altar. The like form was to be observed when any of the laity desired to have any servant of the church promoted to orders, or when the like promotion was petitioned for by the prior of a chapter or of a monastery. This emperor died in 840, and Lotharius, his son, had the title of Emperor. He published a capitulary in Rome, in 842.

In the third chapter of the first part, we find the following expression—

" In electione autem Romani pontificis nullus sive liber, sive servus præsumat aliquod impedimentum facere."

" Let no one whether freeman or slave presume to create any impediment in the election of the Roman pontiff."

Which leads us to suspect that some slaves possessed considerable power or influence.

The second part consists of a portion enacted at a different period, but engrossed with that which I have noticed.

In the second chapter, fines are imposed for creating riots in any church. And the chapter concludes in the following words—

"Et qui non habet unde ad ecclesiam persolvat, tradat se in servitio eidem ecclesiæ, usque dum totum debitum persolvat."

" And let him who has not the means of paying the church, give himself in servitude to that same church until he pays the whole debt."

By the tenth chapter he restrained the power of manumission.

" Quod per xxx annos servus liber fieri non possit, si pater illius servus, aut mater ancilla fuit. Similiter de aldionibus præcipimus."

" That a slave whose father or whose mother was a slave cannot become free before xxx years of age. We order that the same. shall be the case respecting Aldions."

In the xii, he states that these are but a continuance of the laws of his grandfather Charles and of his father Louis. And in Tit. I, 12 of Ulpian, reference is made to a variety of enactments of the ancient Roman law, that a slave manumitted under the age of thirty could not be a Roman citizen except by a special grant of a court.

The xiii, declares that free women who unite with their own slaves are in the royal power, and are given up, together with their children, to slavery amongst the Lombards.

The xiv, enacts, that a free woman who shall unite herself to the male slave of another and remain so for a year and a day, shall together with her children become enslaved to her husband's owner.

The xv, regulates that if the free husband of a free woman shall for crime or debt, bring himself into servitude to another, and she not consent to remain with him, the children are free; but if she die and another free woman, knowing his condition, marries him, the children of this latter shall be slaves.

A number of chapters are also on these records showing the insufficiency of servile testimony. Others provide against the oppression of poor freemen, so that they shall not be easily compelled to sell themselves into slavery.

About the year 860, Pope Nicholas I, sent to the newly converted Christians of Bulgaria, answers to several inquiries which they made for the regulation of their conduct. The 97th regards slaves who accuse their masters to the prince or to the court: and the Pope refers them to the obligation of the master as given in chap. vi of the Epistle of St. Paul to Ephesians : not to use threatenings towards their servants, and then asks, how much more strongly does the spirit of this maxim of kindness and affection bear upon the servant and teach him to be of an humble and forgiving disposition, such as that chapter enjoins ; referring also to the direction of our Saviour, Luke vi, 37, and the injunction of the Apostle 1 Thess. v, 15, for their direction.

I may perhaps here close that part of my observations which were intended to show that by *Scripture* and by *tradition* we discover that the existence of domestic slavery is perfectly compatible with the practice of true religion.

In the Scriptural evidence, we have seen the laws regarding it, made for his chosen people by God himself. We have found that amongst the various crimes denounced by the Saviour, he never directly or indirectly either mentions or alludes to this, yet he not only was fully aware of its existence, but it was alluded to and spoken of by slave-holders, upon whom he conferred great favors and to whose high virtues he bore ample testimony.

His apostles distinctly show their respective duties to the slave-holder and to the slave, who are both members of the church of Jesus Christ, and strongly as they recommended kindness and mercy to one, they inculcate obedience and humility upon the other.

Tradition is the preservation of the original doctrine. It is evinced by a variety of testimony, consisting of documents, of usages, of legislation, of practice, of preaching and so on., I have, for nearly the first nine centuries of the Christian era, that is for the earlier half of that period which has elapsed from the establishment of the Christian religion, shown all this variety of testimony, exhibiting the unchanging doctrine on this subject, preserved under a variety of circumstances in all those regions that had received the light of the gospel.

This, I repeat, is what we call *tradition*. And of what does that body of evidence consist ? Of the admonitions of the earliest and the holiest pastors of the church; of the decrees of her councils, repeatedly made upon a variety of occasions ; of the synodical condemnation of those who, under the pretext of religion, would teach the slave to despise his master ; of the prohibition to her prelates to interfere with the slave property of any one, without his full permission, for the purpose of ordination or of monastic profession ; of the sanction and support of those laws by which the civil power sought to preserve the rights of the owner; of the deeds of gift or of sale by which the church acquired such property for the cultivation of her lands, for the support of her temples, for the maintenance of her clergy, for the benefit of her monasteries, of her hospitals, of her orphans, and of her other works of charity. All this testified that she continued to regard the possession of such property as being fully compatible with the doctrine of the gospel that she was commissioned to proclaim. And whilst she denounced the pirates who made incursions to reduce to bondage those who were free and unoffending, whilst she regarded with just execration the persons who fitted out ships and hired men to engage in such a traffic as is known now by the expression " slave-trade;" she found domestic slavery existing throughout her jurisdiction, and mixed up with almost all her transactions during those centuries from whose records I have quoted so sparingly, though perhaps so tediously, to form an outline of my argument of tradition. Thus, by the testimony of the church, and not by our own conjectures, we learn that doctrine which was originally delivered by God, and then handed down, without alteration, through successive generations.

I now draw your attention to the influence that Mahometanism had upon slavery. In the east the first Arabian warriors who marched as the propagators of Islamism, offered to those whom they assailed the alternative of embracing their religion, or paying them tribute, or taking the chances of war. Persia and Syria were quickly under their yoke. About the year 645 Egypt fell into their hands, and the conquest of Cyprus was not long delayed. In all those places the slaves of Jews and of Christians were admitted to their freedom upon declaring themselves believers in the doctrines of the Koran, and we can easily conceive that in this way great numbers obtained their emancipation. On the other hand many of those who were made captives in war were reduced to slavery, so that it is not improbable that the accounts may be at the least balanced.

There was, however, a serious difference between the position of the slave under the caprice of a barbarian flushed with victory, and taught to consider his servant as an infidel dog, and of one who professed the same religion as his master, and that master taught that at the tribunal of their common God he should account most fully for every injustice or unkindness done to his slave. Nor was this the only restraint imposed upon him. We have seen how, by the canons of the church and the laws of the land, there was ample protection afforded to the weaker party. If to this we add the heavy tribute imposed upon the Christian, and his perpetual liability to insult and injustice, the slave of such a slave must himself be in a worse position than if the owner had been in his former freedom.

I am well aware that some of the writers on history, upon whom it is fashionable to rely, give us glowing descriptions of the noble qualities of the Saracens, and delight to dwell upon the superiority of the polished Mussulman over the rude and superstitious Gothic Christians of this age. Mr. Gibbon is as eloquent as he is imaginative upon the theme. It suited his object, and was naturally to be expected from the writer whose aim was to destroy Christianity by drawing it into contempt. But, fortunately, whosoever will calmly investigate facts, instead of being content with partial, discolored, and deceptive statements, will soon detect the fraud. I have no difficulty in concluding, even after a limited view, that the progress of the Saracen did much to perpetuate and to extend slavery, and to render the situation of its victims much worse than it was at the period of the Hegira.

Sicily was the next foothold of the Saracens, and their first resting-place in Europe, in 655. They threatened Constantinople and Italy, and before the close of the seventh century the Vandal, the Visigoth, and the Moor were subjected to their yoke along the whole range of northern Africa. You, sir, cannot be ignorant of their descent upon Spain, and of their success in the beginning of the next century, when the throne of Roderic was overturned. It may be permitted to me, sir, in this place to give a sketch of the mildness, the magnanimity, and the generosity of this favorite people of the author of the Decline and Fall. I shall merely give an outline of the clemency shown to a country which had submitted to the conquerors' yoke. I translate it from Fleury, liv, xli, par. 25, who refers to authorities of the highest description, by whom he is amply sustained. Toledo was quietly given up to Mousa, the governor of Africa, as vicar to the Caliph; "who put the chief men to death, and subjected all Spain as far as Saragossa, which he found open. He burned the towns, he had the most powerful citizens crucified, he cut the throats of the children and of the infants, and spread terror on every side." I should suppose that the precepts of St. Paul, to treat the Christian slaves with kindness and to forbear threatenings, would produce little effect upon the gentle Saracen!

Sardinia next fell into their power, and they avowed that their object was to seize upon the Vatican, and to allow to the head of the Christians, and to the body over which he presided, as little power as they could, and for as short a space of time as possible.

A few of the Spaniards had taken refuge in the mountains of Asturia, and chose Pelagius, son of Fasila, of the royal family of the Goths, for their prince. Attacked in their place of retreat, this remnant of the Christians defended themselves with valor and kept their borders free. In the east the Christians suffered dreadful persecution, and they who escaped death, and would not apostatize, suffered worse than slavery.

In 719, crossing the Pyrenees, the Mahometans poured themselves upon the south of France. After two years of ravages, Zama, their chief, was compelled by Eude, duke of Aquitain, to raise the siege of Toulouse, he was slain and his troops driven back; but their incursions were repeated, and it is stated by the historians of the time that in one action they lost 375,000 men. It was in an action with them, between Tours and Poictiers, that Charles, the father of Pepin, uniting his forces with those of Eude, gave them a signal defeat, and got the surname of *Martel*, from the *hammering* by which he spread such destruction through their host. Though the French church suffered greatly from their ravages, yet the warriors prevented their carrying off many slaves.

The Christians were allowed to practise their religion in the subjugated portion of Spain, with great restrictions, and upon payment of heavy tribute. Alphonsus the Catholic succeeded Fasila, the son of Pelagius, in 740, and, finding the Mussulman weakened by his losses in France, struck a blow for the liberation of Spain, and recovered a considerable number of towns, releasing tens of thousands of Christians from their bondage.

About fifty years later Alphonsus the chaste conquered a large portion of the Peninsula, and kept up an intercourse with Charlemagne, to whom, upon the conquest of Lisbon in 798, he sent, amongst other presents, seven Moorish slaves.

In 842 the Moorish Mussulmen entered the Rhone, ravaged the south of France, near Arles, and carried off a large booty and several persons into slavery. And here we may fix the origin of that piracy which our government and the governments of Great Britain and France have so lately succeeded in completely destroying, after a duration of about one thousand years.

Italy also was, by the dispute of two chieftains for the possession of Benevento, laid open to them. Radelgise called to his aid the Moors of Africa, and Siconulph those of Spain, both parties accepted the invitations, and each returned with a large booty and many captives. In 846 a Moorish band entered the Tiber, sacked the vicinage of Rome, took Fondi, carried off booty and prisoners, scoured the country south to Gaeta, and defeated a body of French troops sent to capture them. They did not re-embark until the following April, when they were lost in a storm. A number of those who came to Benevento continued in its vicinity, making occasional predatory incursions.

In 849 a company of Moors from Africa came to rendezvous at Tozar, in Sardinia, thence to make an incursion by the Tiber upon Rome. A fleet was fitted out at Naples, Amalfi, and Gaeta to intercept them; this expedition anchored at Ostia, where the pope visited them, celebrated mass, and gave them communion, and returned to Rome. Next day the

Moors hove in sight. The Neapolitans went out to meet them, and made a well-directed assault. The fleets were however separated by a storm, in which the chief part of the Moorish vessels were wrecked. Of those Saracens who got safe to the shore, several were killed in fight, some were hanged, and a large number were brought to Rome, where they were kept enslaved at the public works, and particularly on the walls which were now being built to enclose the Vatican and the church of St. Peter within the city, as this place, having previously been without the walls, had been plundered by the Moors in their piratical incursions in 846.

I have noticed these acts of the Saracens, as I shall the similar ones of the Northmen or Danes, in order to show why, though great efforts were made by many benevolent persons to abolish slavery or to mitigate its evils, those efforts were unsuccessful. I also desired, in giving this brief outline, to exhibit the clear distinction between domestic slavery and the slave trade, and to show that, whilst the church tolerated the one, she always condemned the other.

> I have the honor to be, sir,
> Respectfully, &c.
>
> † JOHN, *Bishop of Charleston.*

CHARLESTON, S. C., *March* 31, 1841.

LETTER XVII.

To THE HON. JOHN FORSYTH, SECRETARY OF STATE, U. S.

SIR—The Christian religion had, in the eighth century, spread through a considerable portion of that territory now known as Germany, and had succeeded in mitigating the evils of slavery in the places where it had its due influence. Scandinavia whose western boundary was the Atlantic or German ocean, lay on both sides of that gulf, called in the phrase of the writers of the ninth and tenth centuries, Mare Balticum and Mare Barbarum, both known in previous ages as the Sinus Codanus, and now as the Baltic sea, the Gulf of Bothnia, and the Gulf of Finland. Its western boundary was that region of then undefined extent and character called Sarmatia. Generally, Scandinavia may be said to comprise Denmark,

Norway and Sweden of the present day. The Cimbri who occupied the present portion of Denmark, known as Jutland, were, I may say, the only portion of the Scandinavian race that was beginning to be known in the days of Charles Martel. Accustomed to the stormy sea that raged and foamed about their coasts, this race of barbarians ventured to a distance in vessels of no mighty formidable size, and in the middle of the eighth century, beginning to find their cold and barren regions fully stocked with inhabitants, ventured upon voyages of discovery. Scotland as being the most convenient, was first troubled with their visits; and, about the year 790, they made a descent upon Ireland, in the reign of Doonchad or Donagh, the successor of Niel Frassach. Their incursion was made upon the small island of Rechran or Ragulin, which they laid waste, in 797. According to the Ulster Annals, they plundered and devastated *Innis Patrick*, now called *Holm Patrick*, carrying away several captives, among whom was a sister of St. Findan:—some time afterwards, he was himself made captive by another party of marauders, but he concealed himself in the cavern of a rock on one of the Orkney islands, where they stopped; and, after their departure, making his way to Scotland, he was able to return home. He was subsequently one of the first monks of the monastery of Rhingaw, in the Duchy of Nassau, and near which he was for many years a recluse. After his death and the belief of his salvation, he was chosen patron of that monastery.

In 793, or the fifth year of Ethelred or Ethelbert on the 7th of June, they commenced the plunder of the fine abbey of Lindisfarne. The following is extracted from Lingard's History of the Anglo Saxon church:

" In the year 793, the inhabitants of Northumbria were alarmed by the appearance of a Danish armament near the coast. The barbarians were permitted to land without opposition. The plunder of the churches exceeded their most sanguine expectations: and their route was marked by the mangled carcases of the nuns, the monks, and the priests, whom they had massacred. But historians have scarcely condescended to notice the misfortunes of other churches: their attention has been absorbed by the fate of Lindisfarne. That venerable pile, once honored by the residence of the apostle of Northumbria, and sanctified by the remains of St. Cuthbert, became the prey of the barbarians. Their impiety polluted the altars, and their rapacity was rewarded by its gold and silver ornaments, the oblations of gratitude and devotion. The monks endeavored by concealment to elude their cruelty; but the greater number were discovered; and were either slaughtered on the island, or drowned in the sea. If the lives of the children were spared, their fate was probably more severe than that of their teachers; they were carried into captivity."

We find also that Charlemagne, in the month of March, 800, visited the German coast, to have proper precautions taken against the incursions and ravages of the Northmen or Danes, who had already plundered several places and carried off captives.

In 802, they made another incursion on Ireland and burned the famous monastery of Hy, and repeated their visit four years after, in 807, penetrating as far as Roscommon; they destroyed the town and ravaged the country, carrying off several captives; but in 812, the Irish made a determined resistance, and after three signal defeats, the Northmen escaped from the island.

This, however, was but a short respite; for, in five years afterwards, the Norwegian Turgesius brought with him an immense force, with which he overran a large portion of the island; his arrival was in 835, but during the twelve previous years, Cork, Lismore, Armagh, Monaghan, Louth, and several other cities and towns, together with their territories, were plundered by those idolaters; the greater portion of their clergy, and monks, and nuns were massacred, many of the inhabitants taken into captivity, and several of the most pious and learned men migrated to the continent, where several of them were elevated to bishoprics, others placed at the head of monasteries, and not a few were employed in the professorships of universities then beginning to be founded.

The horde that accompanied Turgesius was the most numerous and the most savage that had yet appeared; and, within three years, it had nearly overrun Connaught, Leinster, and Ulster. Two large additional fleets brought an immense accession of the savages in 837; one of them entered the river Boyne and the other came up the Liffey; the masses which they poured upon the country, spread in all directions over its surface, committing every kind of excess.

We have a curious exhibition in 848, after Emly had been destroyed by the Northmen: Olchobair Mckinede, who had been abbot and bishop of that see, was made king of Munster, and uniting his troops with those of Dorcan, king of Leinster, was seen leading the armies to victory over the pagans. The archbishop of Armagh, Forannan, who was primate of all Ireland was, however, in this same year, made captive by Turgesius, who sent him, his clergy, and the church furniture, with about seven hundred other captives to Limerick, to be carried into slavery. Melseachlin, king of Ireland, sent ambassadors to make a treaty with Charles the Bald, who then was the successor of Charlemagne upon the throne of France, and who was also harassed by the Scandinavians. Turgesius was defeated by the Irish monarch, made captive, and drowned: the Irish rose on every side upon their oppressors, and nearly drove the barbarians from the

The English Heptarchy, at this time, suffered equally as did Ireland, and with less intermission.

In 850, Dublin was invaded by a large body of Northmen, whom the Irish denominated *Fin-gâl*, or *White Strangers*, and another body called *Dubh-gâl*, or *Black Strangers*, who succeeded in keeping a foothold in Leinster and a part of Ulster, and in making captives.

In the year 835, a large party of them entered the Loire in France, and fixed their head-quarters in the Island of Hero, now called Nourmoutier, whence they made their incursions. The festival of All Saints had long previous to this, probably upwards of two centuries, been in Rome observed on the first of November, as it still continues to be, by a regulation of Pope Boniface IV, who died in 615. From the Chronicle of Sigebert we learn that the Emperor Louis, finding the bishops of France and of Germany anxious to have its observance on the same day, regulated for that purpose with Pope Gregory IV, and being harassed by the incursions of the Scandinavian pirates and of the Saracens, in ordaining the office the following was directed to be sung in the hymn for matins:

> Auferte gentem perfidam,
> Credentium de finibus;
> Ut unus omnes unicum
> Ovile nos Pastor regat.

> Take far away the wicked bands
> Beyond the pale of Christian lands;
> That Christ's one pastor thus may keep
> In but one fold his ransomed sheep.

Hilberd, the abbot of Noirmoutier, applied to Pepin, king of Aquitain, for aid; but as the island was considered indefensible against the pirates, it was decided to withdraw from it the relics of St. Filibert, its patron.

The French writers describe the Danes as now pouring in multitudes upon their northern coasts, to carry away captives into slavery and to load their vessels with booty. On the 12th of May, 841, they entered the Seine, whilst the sons of Louis were yet engaged in their unfortunate broils with each other, and Charles the Bald had become king. Ascending the river they sacked Rouen, burning the monastery of St. Ouen, at that time outside the walls; leaving this place, they burned the monastery of Jumieges; that of Fontanelle was spared upon a ransom, and the monks of St. Denys paid them twenty-six pounds of silver for the ransom of sixty-eight captives. On the last day of May they re-embarked, after having, within nineteen days, devastated an immense region along the banks of this river.

In 843 they ascended the Loire, in the month of June, and took the city of Nantes by escalade. It was at the time filled with the inhabitants of the neighboring country, who had assembled to celebrate the festival of St. John the Baptist, June 24. These retired to the Cathedral, where the bishop and his clergy were, and shut the gates: those the Danes soon burst open, and committed dreadful carnage, carrying off immense booty and some captives, whom they sent to their ships, whither they were followed by some Christians, who brought money to ransom their friends.

In 844 they went farther south, up the Garonne, and pillaged Toulouse. Some, who made an inroad upon Gallicia in Spain, were driven off by the Saracens. In 845 Raigner or Ragner Lodbrog, one of their vikingr or sea-kings, entered the Seine with twenty-six vessels, landed at Rouen in March, and spread terror and devastation on every side. At Chavelanne, near St. Germain-en-Laye, they were informed that the monarch Charles the Bald was marching at the head of an army to attack them; they crossed the river to the side which was but feebly defended, continued their devastations, leaving in their rear several Christians hanging on trees, stakes, and even in the houses. They entered Paris on Easter Saturday, March 28, and found the city and its environs nearly deserted. Charles reluctantly, but with the advice of several of his lords, made a treaty with them, in which they swore by their gods and all that they held sacred not to re-enter his kingdom, except upon his invitation, and he paid them seven thousand pounds of silver.

The pirates, however, after leaving the Seine, ravaged a portion of the sea-coast, and on their homeward voyage were wrecked on the Northumbrian coast, where the survivers, amongst whom was Ragner, began to plunder; but they were attacked by Ælla, who had usurped the throne of that kingdom. The pirate was taken and put to death. Ragner had ten Sons, who vowed to revenge their father's death. At the head of a formidable fleet they approached the coast of East Angles, landed, and lived during winter on free quarters, and in the spring marked their advances to Northumbria in lines of blood and ruin. Ælla fell into their hands and suffered dreadful torture. Berenicia shared the fate of Deira, and during seven years Halfdene was engaged in the work of devastation.

They did not lose sight of Ireland, and in 850 they compelled the monarch Melseachlin to make a treaty with them, by means of which they made several settlements.

In 845 they were defeated in their first enterprise upon Friesland, but, succeeding in two others, they gained a footing also here. An immense body of the Scandinavians sailed up the Elbe with six hundred vessels, large and small, under King Roric. St. Anscarius, archbishop of Hamburg, at first thought to defend that city, but soon saw the folly of the attempt, and withdrew with what he could remove. The city was burned, but several captives were taken through the country. The forces of Roric were now poured upon Saxony. But they met a signal defeat, and their leader, learning the disasters of Ragner, sent messengers to Paderborn, where Louis, king of Germany, was then holding an assembly of his states, and was receiving to his alliance the people of Sclavonia and Bulgaria, who sent deputies to request that they might be also instructed in the Christian doctrine. The Scandinavians sued for peace, which they received upon the release of the persons whom they had taken to be their slaves, and the return of what booty they had.

The zeal of the holy archbishop of Hamburg had previously prompted him to send missionaries into Scandinavia, to instruct those barbarians in the Christian religion, but Gausbert, whom he had consecrated bishop to carry the light of truth into Sweden, was with his companions driven thence by the people, after having been robbed of whatever goods they had.

The Normans, who succeeded in Friesland, proceeded by that side into France. Flanders fell under their assaults. Another division, in 848, sailing up the Garonne, laid siege to Bordeaux, which was betrayed into their hands by the Jews. After ravaging Aquitain, they went to the district of Poictiers, or Poictou, whence they carried great booty. Roric, with his followers, after leaving the Elbe, went to the Rhine and the Scheldt, destroyed the monasteries as far as Ghent, and the Emperor Lothaire, being unable to subdue him, was content to receive him as his vassal, and gave him the large tract of territory which he had previously occupied. Godfrey, another of their chieftains, repulsed in an attack upon England, sailed up the Seine in 850, and after some achievements obtained from Charles a territory round Beauvais in 850. Thus did the Northmen begin to make permanent settlements in the more southern regions of Europe, and an opportunity was thus given of bringing them to civilization and to Christianity. The history of this period, however, is a calamitous series of recitals of devastation committed by successive hordes of Northmen and armies and squadrons of Saracens, upon those churches which had begun to be reduced to discipline, after the centuries of war and plunder by the Huns, the Goths, and the Vandals.

In 856 and 857 Paris and all the region between it and the British Channel were plundered with impunity, as also nearly all the region on the Atlantic coast of France as far in as Orleans; the churches, as usual, were either sacked or redeemed, and multitudes of captives carried away to slavery. This necessarily destroyed all notion of justice and all peace, and the capitularies of the monarchs, as well as the canons of the councils, exhibit the ruin of morality. We find, in 850, the greater number of the prelates and chief men of the vicinity of Flanders slain or in captivity. We find the pirates had circumnavigated Spain, entered the gulf of Lyons, committed depredations in Provence, and made incursions upon Italy; and in 861 the Seine was again infested, and Paris was terrified by seeing the Northmen at her gates, and two years afterwards the kingdom was scandalized by the apostacy of Pepin, the nephew of Charles and son of Pepin, king of Aquitain, who had become a monk, and, when his father's realms were ravaged by this horde, publicly renounced the Christian religion, embraced their idolatry, and joined their forces. He was subsequently taken by his uncle's troops, recanted his errors, did public penance, and returned to his monastery.

In 883, after the death of Louis, king of Germany, and the withdrawing of the troops who kept the Normans in check, they poured themselves on both sides of the Rhine as high up as Coblentz ; they overran Flanders, and made a stable of the fine chapel of Charlemagne, at Aix-la-Chapelle: —a favorite usage of the French revolutionary soldiers about forty or fifty years ago ; I have seen some of the finest churches in France and Italy which those desecrators of the holy name of liberty had thus profaned. The Emperor Charles the Bald, returning from Italy, besieged a large body of them in a fortified camp near the Rhine. A treaty was made, and Godfrey with his band besought baptism, and received the duchy of Friesland. Sigefrey, the other chieftain, promised peace upon receiving a large contribution.

Alfred, known, and deservedly so, as the Great, was the youngest of five sons of Ethelwulf, king of Wessex, and was born in 849. At the age of five years his father declared him king of a portion of his dominions, and sent him to Rome, where he received the sacrament of confirmation and the regal unction from Pope Leo IV. Two years afterwards Ethelwulf himself went to the holy see, taking Alfred with him. In 872 Alfred became king of Wessex, upon the death of his brother Ethelred. This is not the place to dwell upon the history of his disasters or of his virtues. You are aware of his being obliged to conceal himself in the morasses of Somersetshire, and of the almost miraculous manner in which an opportunity was subsequently afforded him of placing himself at the head of a body of his faithful followers, and how victory after victory enabled him to free his people from the Danish yoke. Gothrun, the Dane, submitted, and was received upon conditions, one of which was to embrace the Christian religion. He was instructed, and baptized by the name of Athelstan, Alfred himself being his sponsor. And, as Lingard remarks, " the followers of Guthrun gradually adopted the habits of civ-ilized life; and, by acquiring an interest in the soil, contributed to pro-tect it from the ravages of subsequent adventurers."

Alfred applied himself to revise the laws, to protect and to re-establish religion. He was a most pious and exemplary monarch. He created a navy, seeing that it must be the best natural bulwark of the island; he instituted the mode of trial by jury; he was also a patron of literature, which he sought to restore and to extend.

France was during this period so completely overrun by the pagans in many places that thousands of Christians, to escape death or bondage, publicly renounced their religion and embraced the pagan rites. We have however an interesting account of the resistance made by Paris, which then only occupied the island in the Seine, to the passage of their vessels. The Emperor Charles the Fat had confided it to Gozlin, its bishop, and he not only animated the people to its defence, but fought at their head with his nephew Ebolus, an abbot, Odo, Eude, count of Paris, and Robert his brother. The Normans continued the siege for many months, until the last day of January, 886, when they turned the siege into a blockade, which continued during a year. The Normans carried their vessels two miles over land beyond the city, and sailed up, ravaging the country. The emperor at last relieved the city by a dishonorable peace.

In 893 a fleet of three hundred and thirty sail assembled in the port of Boulogne, in France, under the command of Hastings, one of the most renowned of the sea-kings, for the purpose of conquering for him a king-dom in Britain. By force and stratagem they, during three years, con-tended against Alfred; and in place of being sustained against them by the Danes, to whom he gave a settlement in his dominions, he discovered that most of them took advantage of his position to return to the work of plunder. Alfred, by patience, by exertion, and by tactics, subdued them all, restored their prisoners, and obtained from Hastings a promise to leave the island for ever. Returning to France, this chief made incursions from the banks of the Seine, and before the close of the century, making a treaty with King Charles the Simple, he obtained the city of Chartres and the adjoining territory.

Having thus brought to your view the situation of England, of France, and of the Low Countries under the Northmen, to the close of the ninth century, I return to Ireland.

In 853 a sea-king, who is indifferently styled Amlave, Auliffe, and Olave, accompanied by his two brothers, Sitric and Ivar, arrived in Ire-land from Norway with additional forces, and was acknowledged chief-

tain by all the Northmen in the island. Auliffe took possession of Dublin,
which he enlarged. Ivar settled in Limerick, which he greatly improved,
and Sitric began the building of Waterford. War raged between them
and the Irish, and between parties of the Danes against each other, and
intestine divisions existed also amongst the Irish, so that carnage and
slavery for years devastated the island. The success was various. In
860 Melseachlin, the king, defeated Auliffe with great slaughter, and nine
years subsequently this latter plundered Armagh, burned its sacred edifices, and took a large number of captives. In the next year the two
brothers, Auliffe and Ivar, made a descent upon Scotland, and burned
Dunbarton. Auliffe died soon after his return in 871, and was succeeded
by Ivar, who died in 873. In 884 they plundered Kildare, and carried
away nearly 300 captives to their ships. In 895 Armagh was again devastated, and 710 captives carried away ; soon after this the Danes were
defeated and driven from Dublin by the men of Bregh, headed by Maol-
Finia, the son of Flanagan, and by the Leinster forces, commanded by
Carrol. In other parts of the island they also, at this period, suffered
great defeats.

Not the least curious of the discoveries which are made from a perusal
of the ancient documents which remain to us, is the wonderful disposition
by which Divine Providence causes even the crimes of men to be made sub-
servient to the ends of mercy. In examining the way in which the Irish
who had been carried into slavery by the Northmen were distributed, I
see that, although Iceland did not generally receive nor long retain the
truths of the gospel, yet they were published therein by some of the Irish
captives that were carried thither by the Norwegians in this century.
They who desire more information on the subject can consult Lanigan's
Ecclesiastical History of Ireland, vol. iii, c. 20, § 4, and c. xxii, § 2.

I cannot, sir, better conclude this letter than by submitting to you the
following remarks of the learned historian, Dr. Lingard, taken from chap.
xxi of his " Antiquities of the Anglo-Saxon Church."

" The numerous massacres of the war had considerably thinned the
population of the country ; and, to supply the deficiency, Alfred had
adopted an obvious but inadequate expedient, in the naturalization of several thousand Danes. In every county the strangers were intermixed
with the natives. In East-Anglia and Northumbria their numbers greatly
exceeded the descendants of the ancient inhabitants. If the sacred rite
of baptism had entitled the barbarians to the appellation and privileges of
Christians, their manners and notions still reduced them to a level with
their pagan brethren. The superstition of Scandinavia was in many
places restored. The charms and incantations of magic amused the cre-

dulity of the people; the worship of Odin was publicly countenanced, or clandestinely preserved; and oaths and punishments were often employed in vain to extort from these nominal converts an external respect for the institutions of Christianity. The morals of many among the Anglo-Saxons were scarcely superior to those of the naturalized Danes. During the long and eventful contest the administration of justice had been frequently suspended; habits of predatory warfare had introduced a spirit of insubordination; and impunity had strengthened the impulse of the passions. To the slow and tranquil profits of industry, were preferred the violent but sudden acquisitions of rapine : the roads were infested with robbers; and the numbers and audacity of the banditti compelled the more peaceable inhabitants to associate for the protection of their lives, families, and property. The dictates of natural equity, the laws of the gospel, and the regulations of ecclesiastical discipline were despised. The indissoluble knot of marriage was repeatedly dissevered at the slightest suggestion of passion or disgust; and in defiance of divine and human prohibitions, the nuptial union was frequently polluted and degraded by the unnatural crime of incest. To reform the degeneracy of his subjects, Alfred published a new code of laws, extracted from those of his predecessors and of the Jewish legislator; and the execution of forty-four judges in one year shows both the inflexible severity of the king and the depravity of those whose duty it was to be the guardians of national morals. That his efforts were attended with partial success is not improbable; but, from the complaints and improvements of later legislators, it is evident that it required a succession of several generations before the ancient spirit of licentiousness could be suppressed and extinguished."

This, sir, though written only for the state of England, is, by parity of circumstances, fairly applicable to the greater portion of the Christian world at that period. Of that, however, more hereafter.

I have the honor to be, sir,

Respectfully, &c.

† JOHN, *Bishop of Charleston.*

CHARLESTON, S. C., *April* 8, 1840.

LETTER XVIII.

To the Hon. JOHN FORSYTH, Secretary of State, U. S.

Sir,—In continuing to exhibit the outline of the ravages committed by the Northmen and the Saracens, my object is to show the grounds upon which I shall explain, why so many ages passed away subsequently to the promulgation of Christianity, before Christendom was delivered from the evils of predatory incursions, and the extensive prevalence of domestic slavery. In reviewing history, it is folly to substitute speculation for the recital of facts; and it is upon this ground that I prefer the tedious recital which I give, to getting through in a couple of dashing letters, which would give less information to the understanding, though they might be better calculated to glitter before the imagination.

We have seen, that nearly all the Northern coast of France was, if not in possession, yet at least in the power of the Danes or Northmen, at the close of the ninth century. Many of them, yielding to the zeal of some of the clergy, had embraced the Christian religion; and amongst those who were most devoted to their instruction was Hervey, Archbishop of Rheims, who consulted Pope John X, upon the subject. Charles the simple, finding himself unable to repress their incursions, by the advice of his nobles, treated with them; Francon, Archbishop of Rouen, was the mediator. Charles gave in full fee to Rollo, the Danish chief, all that province thenceforth known as Normandy and his daughter Gisle, as his spouse. Rollo promised to become a Christian, and to do homage as a vassal of the crown of France for the Dukedom, of what was subsequently known as Britanny. In 912, having been instructed by Francon, Rollo was baptized by the name of Robert, and married Gisle, the daughter of Charles III, or the simple. The greater number of his leading officers, following the example of their chief, were instructed, baptized and made alliance with the Franks. Normandy and Britanny became thus in some measure settled, but it took many years to bring other parts of the country into a similar position. Even in Britanny, as late as 942, we find civil war, conspiracy, and treason fomented by Pagans, who sought to subdue those that professed Christianity. In 943, William Longsword, Duke of Normandy, was thus slain by Arnold, Count of Flanders. Hugh, Duke of France, was engaged in almost continual war with a large body of Pagans who occupied Evreux and the

surrounding regions. Louis IV, or the Foreigner, (D'outre mer) had severe contests with Tourmond, a Norman apostate, who sought to bring
Richard, son of William Longsword and his Normans back to idolatry, and
who for this purpose, had formed an alliance with one of the Northmen
chiefs, called Sethric, or Sithric, who probably was one of those in Ireland.
The confusion and barbarity of the times was, not a little, aided by the
scandals of some of the prelates, who had been either placed in their seats
or protected upon them by the warriors of the day, who were often enemies
of religion.

In England, after the death of Alfred in 901, there continued peace for
some time, but Ethelwold, the nephew of this monarch, having disputed the
succession with Edward, the son of Alfred, and finding himself the weaker,
had recourse to the Danes then settled in Northumbria, but they were defeated in their efforts to sustain him and the unfortunate aspirant himself
was slain. "After the death of Ethelwold," writes Lingard, "five years
elapsed without any important act of hostility : in 910, Edward conducted
his forces into Northumbria and spent five weeks in ravaging the country,
and collecting slaves and plunder. The next year, the Northmen returned
the visit."

After many minor efforts, the great contest for the possession of England
took place in 937, between Aulaff the Dane and Athelstan, the grandson
of Alfred, and after terrible carnage, it was decided in favor of the latter
at Brunanburgh, in Northumbria; by this result, Athelstan became in re-
ality the first king of England. Louis IV, of France, was son of Charles
the Simple, by his wife Edgiva, the sister of Athelstan : when Charles was
cast into prison by the treachery of Herbert, Count of Vermandois, the
Queen of France fled to her brother in England, who became the protector
of her son Louis, during thirteen years, whence this latter received the surname of *D'Outre mer*.

Athelstan died in 940, having done much to perfect the institutions
which Alfred had re-established or founded and improved. He was succeeded by Edmund, with whom Auliffe or Aulaff, who had for some time
been settled in Dublin, Ireland, contended, as he had done with his
brother and predecessor Athelstan, for the dominion of England.
The Dane was more successful against Edmund than he had been against
Athelstan, but he died in 941, and Edward recovered the territory over
which his father had held dominion. He was assassinated in 946. His
widow Edgiva, is said to have been a princess of exemplary virtue, whose
solicitude for the relief of the indigent, and charity in purchasing the liberty of slaves, amongst other acts of piety, have been highly extolled by
our ancient writers."*

* Lingard's History of England, ch. iv.

We have seen that in Ireland, in 902, the Northmen who had possession
of Dublin and other parts of Leinster, were defeated and expelled by the
people of that province under the command of Carroll, and by the men of
Bregh under Maol Finia, who subsequently became a monk in Holmpat-
rick, and died in the reputation of great sanctity in 903.   They however
returned, about ten years later, and a party that landed at Waterford, in
914, were put to the sword.   Another division, however, succeeded in
plundering Cork, Lismore and Aghadoe: and about the year 916, they were
again in possession of Dublin, and ravaged a large portion of Leinster,
killing Angare Mac Olioll, king of that province.   They were attacked
near Dublin, in 919, by Niell Glunndubh, king of Ireland, but they made
a desperate resistance under the command of their chiefs Ivar and Sitric:
the Irish monarch was slain together with several of his choice nobles and
the flower of his army.   In the next year, Donogh who succeeded Niell,
avenged the death of his father, but though the barbarians were signally
defeated, yet we find them in 921 march under the command of their
King Godfrey, from Dublin to Armagh and plunder the city; and here is
also the first instance in which we perceive, in Ireland, the churches and
the officiating clergy to have been spared; this leads to the supposition,
that there must have been in that band several who had embraced the
Christian religion either in France or in England, or perhaps in both
countries.

In 925, Aulaff or Auliffe, a son of Sitric, king of Northumbria, flying
before Athelstan, went to Ireland where he found many of his friends; we
find also another Auliffe there, who is called son of Godfred, though perhaps it may be the same, and that his father took the name of Godfred in
place of Sitric.   He with a number of others committed several depredations in nearly all parts of the island for more than twenty years.   In 947
and 948, they suffered two severe defeats from Congall II, in the latter of
which, their King Blacar and the most efficient of his army were slain.   It
is conjectured by the historians of the day, that those defeats caused a
large body of them, for the first time in Ireland, to offer themselves as converts to Christianity.   Be the cause what it may,—the fact is well established that in this year, large bodies of the Northmen in Ireland embraced
the Christian religion, though many of them retained their predatory habits;
as the subsequent history of the island proves.

But that which most forcibly strikes the observer is the fact that not only in Ireland, but in France, in England and Flanders, the new converts
to the faith appear to have been but little changed as a body, so far as regarded their piratical habits.   Occasionally, indeed, we find that their conduct to their captives was not so cruel, and sometimes they spared the

edifices of religion and the clergy. Nor was it only in those regions which they invaded, that they assumed the Christian name. Zealous missionaries had been also labouring during the entire of the tenth century in their own northern cradle, and though encountering formidable difficulties yet were their efforts in the holy cause crowned with no inconsiderable success; and though fleets were fitted out, expeditions undertaken and invasions made, still there was some little mitigation of the attendant evils. From 980 to the close of the century, their incursions and conflicts desolated England, especially under Sweyn and Olave in 995, this latter had already embraced the doctrines of Christianity; when he and his associate had convened for sixteen thousand pounds to withdraw their troops; Olave accompanied two prelates to Andover, where he received the Sacrament of Confirmation from the Bishop of Winchester, and promised Ethelred, who then was the English monarch, never again to draw his sword against his Christian brethren. He kept the pledge and returning to Norway, engaged in efforts to convert his subjects until he was slain by Sweyn. In 1001 a party of the Northmen from the opposite shores of France committed great depredations on the South-Western parts of Ethelred's dominions. In the next year by the intervention of Pope John XV, through his legate Leo, assistant bishop of Treves, the first written treaty extant between an English king and a foreign prince, was made, to establish lasting peace between Ethelred and Richard, Duke or Marquis of Normandy; this was sealed by the marriage of Ethelred, then a widower, with Emma daughter of Richard; but the neglect with which Ethelred treated his young queen, and an atrocious massacre which he planned and executed on the 13th of November of the same year, destroyed all prospect of harmony. On this day, by pre-concert, the Saxons rose upon the Danes throughout the island and a general massacre took place, not only of pagans but of Christians; not only of those who had settled by force in the island, but of those who had been legally naturalized; amongst the victims was Gunhilda, the sister of Sweyn, who had embraced Christianity and married Palig a naturalized northman. Sweyn, during the next four years, ravaged the country in revenge and did not cease until he got thirty-six thousand pounds of silver. He, keeping the letter of his treaty, violated its spirit, for though he remained at home, he secretly permitted Turchill to proceed with a fleet to renew the depredations. Canterbury amongst other places was taken, from which, after great massacre, eight hundred captives were reserved for bondage or ransom; the primate Elphege was kept during several weeks prisoner in expectation of a ransom of three thousand pounds, and as he refused to send to his clergy or to his friends for the money, he was put to death on Easter Saturday, whilst preaching to his captors.

The Northman then for a sum of forty-eight thousand pounds sold his services to the king of England, and many of his followers accepted settlements in the island, whilst the crews of forty-five ships swore allegiance to the English monarch. It is useless to exhibit the struggles subsequently between Ethelred and Sweyn, the contests between Edmund Ironsides and Canute the Dane. It will suffice to state that in 1017, Canute became the monarch of England, confirming his possession of the throne by his nuptials with Emma, the widow of Ethelred. In the laws which this monarch published, is a severe ordinance against the custom of sending *Christians* to be sold into slavery in foreign countries, thereby exposing them to the danger of falling into paganism. Upon the death of Canute, Harold, one of his illegitimate sons, took possession of the English throne. Alfred, a half-brother of Edmund Ironsides, came from Normandy in the hope of being able to compete with him, but was seized upon, on the night after he had landed, together with his followers,—some were liberated, some were condemned to slavery and the others put to cruel deaths. Edward the Confessor succeeded, and thus was the Saxon line re-instated upon Harold's death. This pious monarch restored as far as he could, the dominion of law, mitigated the oppression of the slave and of the vassal, and strove to extend the influence of religion : he also did much to place the liberty of the subject upon a solid basis. Harold filled up the short interval which marks the period from the death of Edward to the battle of Hastings, in which William, Duke of Normandy, a descendant of Rollo, by a desperate effort won the throne of England, and Harold perished in the field, and thus a new order of government commences under the successful descendant of the Northmen.

I shall here copy from the Appendix I, of Dr. Lingard's History of England, his general description of slavery in England under the Anglo-Saxon dynasties.

" The several classes, whose manners have been hitherto described, constituted the Anglo-Saxon nation. They alone were possessed of liberty, or power, or property. They formed, however, but a small part of the population, of which, perhaps, not less than two-thirds existed in a state of slavery. That all the first adventurers were freemen, there can be little doubt; but in the course of their conquests it is probable that they found, it is certain that they made a great number of slaves. The posterity of these men inherited the lot of their fathers: and their number was continually increased by the free-born Saxons, who had been reduced to the same condition by debt, or had been made captives in war, or had been deprived of liberty in punishment of their crimes, or had spontaneously surrendered it to escape the horrors of want. The degradation and enslavement of a freeman were performed before a competent number of witnesses. The unhappy man laid on the ground his sword and his lance, the symbols of the free, took up the bill and the goad, the implements of slavery, and falling on his knees, placed his head in token of submission under the hands of his master.

"All slaves were not, however, numbered in the same class. In the more ancient laws we find the esne distinguished from the theow; and read of female slaves of the first, the second, and the third rank. In later enactments we meet with bordars, cocksets, parddings, and other barbarous denominations, of which, were it easy, it would be useless to investigate the meaning.—The most numerous class consisted of those, who lived on the land of their lord, near to his mansion, called in Saxon his tune, in Latin his villa. From the latter word they were by the Normans denominated villeins, while the collection of cottages in which they dwelt, acquired the name of village. Their respective services were originally allotted to them according to the pleasure of their proprietor. Some tilled his lands, others exercised for him the trades to which they had been educated. In return they received certain portions of land with other perquisites, for the support of themselves and their families. But all were alike deprived of the privileges of freemen. They were forbidden to carry arms. Their persons, families, and goods of every description, were the property of their lord.—He could dispose of them as he pleased, either by gift or sale: he could annex them to the soil or remove them from it: he could transfer them with it to a new proprietor, or leave them by will to his heirs. Out of the hundreds of instances preserved by our ancient writers, one may be sufficient. In the charter by which Harold of Buckenhale gives his manor of Spalding to the abbey of Croyland, he enumerates among its appendages Colgrin his bailiff, Harding his smith, Lefstan his carpenter, Elstan his fisherman, Osmund his miller, and nine others, who probably were husbandmen; and these with their wives and children, their goods and chattels, and the cottages in which they live, he transfers in perpetual possession to the abbey.

"It should, however, be observed, that the hardships of their condition were considerably mitigated by the influence of their religion. The bishop was appointed the protector of the slaves within his diocese; and his authority was employed in shielding them from oppression. Their lords were frequently admonished that slave and freemen were of equal value in the eye of the Almighty: that both had been redeemed at the same price; and that the master would be judged with the same rigour as he had exercised towards his dependants. In general, the services of the slave were fixed and certain: if he performed them faithfully, he was allowed to retain his savings, and many of those who cultivated portions of land, or had received permission to exercise their trades in the burghs, acquired a comparative degree of opulence, which enabled them to purchase their liberty from the kindness or avarice of their lords. Even the laws suppose some kind of property in the slave, since they allow him to commute the legal punishment of whipping for a fine of six shillings, and fix the relief of a villein on a farm at the price of his best beast.

" The prospect of obtaining their freedom was a powerful stimulus to industry and good behaviour.—Besides those who were able to purchase it themselves, many obtained it from the bounty of benefactors.—Some were emancipated by the justice and gratitude of their masters: others owed their freedom to motives of religion. When the celebrated Wilfrid had received from Edelwalch, king of Sussex, the donation of the isle of Selsey, with two hundred and fifty male and female slaves, the bishop instructed them in the christian faith, baptized them, and immediately made them free. Their manumission was an act of charity frequently inculcated by the preachers: and in most of the wills, which are still extant, we meet with directions for granting liberty to a certain number of slaves. But the commiseration of the charitable was more excited by the condition of *wite theow* (those who had been reduced to slavery by a judicial sentence) than of such as had been born in that state, and had never tasted the blessings of liberty. By the bishops in the council of Calcuith it was agreed to free at their decease every slave of that description; and similar provisions are inserted in the wills of the lady Wynfleda, of Athelstan, son of king Ethelred, and of Ælfric, archbishop of Canterbury. Their manumission, to be legal, was to be performed in public, in the market, in the court of the hundred, or in the church at the foot of the principal altar. The lord taking the hand of the slave offered it to the bailiff, sheriff, or clergyman, gave him a sword and a lance, and told him that the ways were open, and that he was at liberty to go wheresoever he pleased.

" Before I conclude this subject, it is proper to add that the sale and purchase of slaves publicly prevailed during the whole of the Anglo-Saxon period. These unhappy men were sold like cattle in the market; and there is reason to believe that a slave was usually estimated at four times the price of an ox. To the importation of foreign slaves no impediment had ever been opposed: the export of native slaves was forbidden under severe penalties. But habit and the pursuit of gain had taught the Northumbrians to bid defiance to all the efforts of the legislature. Like the savages of Africa, they are said to have carried off, not only their own countrymen, but even their friends and relatives; and to have sold them as slaves in the ports of the continent. The men of Bristol were the last to abandon this nefarious traffic. Their agents travelled into every part of the country; they were instructed to give the highest price for females in the state of pregnancy: and the slave ships regularly sailed from that port to Ireland, where they were secure of a ready and profitable market. Their obstinacy yielded, however, not to the severity of the magistrates, but to the zeal of Wulstan, bishop of Worcester. That prelate visited Bristol several years successively, resided for months together in the neighbourhood, and preached on every Sunday against the barbarity and irreligion of the dealers in slaves. At last the merchants were convinced by his reasons, and in that gild solemnly bound themselves to renounce the trade. One of the members was soon after tempted to violate his engagement. His perfidy was punished with the loss of his eyes.

" We have still to consider a class of men, partly free, and partly slaves, the inhabitants of the cities, burghs and ports, which were the property sometimes of one, sometimes of several opulent individuals. The burghers were in general tradesmen and mechanics, divided into two classes: the one of men who held their houses by a fixed rent, and were at liberty to quit them when they pleased; the other of villeins, or the descendants of villeins, who had been permitted to migrate from the country for the benefit of trade, and lived in houses which were considered as portions of the manors to which the original settlers had belonged.—The burghers were still annexed to the soil, and transferable with it; and were still compelled to do service in like manner with their brethren in the country. But all possessed superior advantages. They were better protected from the attack of an enemy; they enjoyed the benefit of a market for the sale of their wares.—They formed gilds or corporations, which guaranteed the good conduct of their members, and were under the government of the reeve or chief lord. But the privileges and burthens, the customs and services of the inhabitants of different burghs, and frequently of those in the same burgh, were so various, complex, and contradictory, that it is impossible to arrange them under distinct heads, or to describe them with accuracy.—They originated in the wants, the caprice, the favour of the several proprietors; and those who desire a more ample gratification of their curiosity on this subject must have recourse to the authentic pages of Domesday.''

In Ireland, after the conversion of the Northmen had commenced, as we have previously seen, in the year 948, we have nearly a repetition of the former scenes of turmoil, until the power and spirit of this formidable and restless race were broken at Clontarf, near Dublin, on the 23d of

April, (Good Friday) in the year 1014, when they suffered an irrecovera-
ble defeat from the Irish forces under the command of the celebrated monarch, Brian Boroimhe, who at the age of 88 years drew up his troops in
good order and led them to victory.   Though in its results Ireland had to
rejoice in the perfect overthrow of those ruthless invaders, yet had she to
weep over the bodies of Brian, of his son Morogh, who fell in the 63d year
of his age, and of his grandson Turlogh, together with those of a host of
the nobility and most valiant warriors who fell for the liberation of their
country.

Here, Sir, I shall close what I had to remark of the impediments created
in England and in Ireland to the progress of religion and the mitigation of
slavery by the piratical Northmen. I shall have still to unfold more of the
difficulties upon the continents of Europe and of Asia.

I have the honor to be, Sir,

Respectfully, &c.,

† JOHN, <i>Bishop of Charleston.</i></div>

CHARLESTON, S. C. <i>April 23d,</i> 1840.

LETTERS

OF THE LATE

BISHOP ENGLAND

TO

THE HON. JOHN FORSYTH,

ON THE

SUBJECT OF DOMESTIC SLAVERY:

TO WHICH ARE PREFIXED

COPIES, IN LATIN AND ENGLISH,

OF THE

POPE'S APOSTOLIC LETTER,

CONCERNING

𝔗𝔥𝔢 𝔄𝔣𝔯𝔦𝔠𝔞𝔫 𝔖𝔩𝔞𝔳𝔢 𝔗𝔯𝔞𝔡𝔢,

WITH SOME INTRODUCTORY REMARKS, ETC.

WIPF & STOCK · Eugene, Oregon

Wipf and Stock Publishers
199 W 8th Ave, Suite 3
Eugene, OR 97401

Letters of the Late Bishop England to the Honorable John Forsyth
on the Subject of Domestic Slavery
To Which Are Prefixed Copies, in Latin and English of the
Pope's Apostolic Letter, Concerning the African Slave Trade,
with Some Introductory Remarks, etc.
By England, John
ISBN 13: 978-1-60608-097-9
Publication date 7/22/2008
Previously published by John Murphy, 1844